Postmodernism
101

POSTMODERNISM 101

A First Course for the Curious Christian

Heath White

BrazosPress
Grand Rapids, Michigan

© 2006 by Heath White

Published by Brazos Press
a division of Baker Publishing Group
P.O. Box 6287, Grand Rapids, MI 49516-6287
www.brazospress.com

Second printing, March 2007

Printed in the United States of America

Library of Congress Cataloging-in-Publication Data
White, Heath, 1972–
   Postmodernism 101 : a first course for the curious Christian / Heath
White.
      p.   cm.
   Includes bibliographical references (p.   ).
   ISBN 10: 1-58743-153-X (pbk.)
   ISBN 978-1-58743-153-1 (pbk.)
      1. Postmodernism—Religious aspects—Christianity. I. Title.
BR115.P74W55 2006
149′.9702427—dc22   2005032404

Contents

Acknowledgments

Eric Sanzone inspired me to write this book; I hope he enjoys it. The manuscript was a long time gestating, and I owe much to the generous assistance of others. Drafts of the manuscript were read and critiqued by Steve Cox, Mel Piehl, Mark Schwehn, Michael Straight, Sandra Visser, Jeff Zalar, and the students of my fall 2004 postmodernism class at Valparaiso University: Karl Aho, Tim Alles, Rachel Carnes, Matt Gotzh, Jon Hallemeier, Bryant Isaacson, Mark Koschmann, Erin Maloney, Tami McDunn, Jeff Murphy, Isaac Schoepp, and Kathryn Veryser. My earnest desire is that this book gives back as much as has been given to it.

Unless the Lord builds the house, they labor in vain that build it.

Why Read about Postmodernism?

I wrote this book because I kept hearing the words "post-modern" and "postmodernism" thrown around in Christian circles. I would read about postmodern church services, or apologetics in a postmodern age, or that we can't compromise with postmodernism. At the same time, I kept running into Christians who wanted to understand these discussions but couldn't, because they didn't know what postmodernism was. Other acquaintances of mine knew something about postmodernism and wanted to think more deeply about what it meant for contemporary Christianity but couldn't, because their knowledge of postmodernism was lightweight, sketchy, or confused.

Here, I thought, I could help. I am a professional philosopher and a Christian, and I wrote this book to help my fellow believers understand and grapple with postmodernism and some of the issues it raises for Christianity in the twenty-first century. I have tried to explain postmodernism, what it is and where it came from, at a reasonably deep level. My hope is that Christians who want to think intelligently about postmodernism and its consequences for the contemporary church will be helped by what's said in these pages.

Although I have a great deal of sympathy for, and attraction to, the high-church denominations, it will be clear before long that my own background is in the low-church, evangelical wing of Protestant Christianity. Probably this work will speak most clearly to believers from a similar background simply because that's what I know best. (I can remove one point of potential confusion right away. My Catholic friends tell me that when they hear the word "church," they think of the hierarchy: bishops, the Roman curia, the pope. I will be using the word in a different sense, either to mean "the body of believers" or "local congregation.") Moreover, I have focused on the concerns that postmodernism raises for evangelical Protestants, since I am best equipped to address those concerns, rather than the concerns of, say, Roman Catholics. However, much of what I have to say should be useful for any Christian person, and I have tried not to exclude or offend members of any branch of Christianity. So whether you are an evangelical Protestant, mainline Protestant, Roman Catholic, Orthodox, or some other variety of Christian, I hope this book will be helpful to you.

What Is Postmodernism?

The word "postmodernism" first surfaced in architecture and the fine arts, perhaps in the 1950s, referring to a new style. Later it acquired a meaning in the world of literature as well. Thus, if an architect, an artist, or an English professor had written this book, it would have a somewhat different emphasis. Sometimes the term is used specifically for the philosophies of a few French thinkers, and if those thinkers had heavily influenced this book's author, its emphasis would be different yet again. As it stands, I will be using "postmodernism" throughout this book in the broadest possible sense, to name a mind-set, a worldview, or a family of similar worldviews, a set of perspectives shared by many people who have come of age rather recently. Postmodernism is not a theory or a creed: it is more like an attitude or a way of looking at things. It didn't drop out of the sky—it showed up at this juncture in history, in Western culture, for specific reasons that have to do with the history of the West. Nor is it, as it is sometimes caricatured, an incoherent jumble—it has weaknesses but also strengths as a way of looking at the world. Nor is it incomprehensibly profound, out of reach of the ordinary layperson. It is a view of the world that, like most other views of the world, requires some effort and sympathy to understand. But it turns on just a few key ideas that can be grasped readily enough.

We can distinguish postmodernism, a worldview, from *postmodernity*, which is a historical era, like the Renaissance or the Bronze Age and which is involved with postmodernism in a complicated cause-and-effect relationship. Consequently, explaining postmodernism will involve pointing out some salient features of postmodernity. The intellectual and historical aspects of being postmodern are wrapped up together; neither can be fully understood without the other.

A warning: this book is short, and it deals with ideas too complex to put on the back of a postcard. I have to paint with a broad brush, sometimes a very broad brush. Everything I write, including this sentence, should ideally be prefaced with "Generally . . ." or "Broadly speaking. . . ." Instead of constantly encumbering you with these caveats, however, I'll just warn you once, here at the beginning, that everything could be said more carefully and precisely. A broad brush makes mistakes easily. The idea, however, is to get the big picture, and that, I believe, I have rendered faithfully enough.

Ideas and Cultures

"Culture" is a grab-bag label for the dominant attitudes, institutions, and practices in a society. Clothing fashions; attitudes toward government; customs surrounding marriage, death, and meals; transportation technology; sexual taboos—all these things and many more make up a culture. Cultures are to people what water is to fish, and thus it can be hard to get a grip on just how pervasive your own culture is in your life. Learning to think in terms of culture is therefore something of an achievement. The idea of culture, however, will play a major role in this book, for it is precisely as a major cultural shift that postmodernism is making its sweeping impact.

Ideas often drive cultures: really big shifts in ideas are really big cultural shifts. This is not to deny that other things, such as new technology and wars, can change a culture too, often by changing the big ideas in the culture. This book will deal with two tectonic movements in ideas, two truly major developments in intellectual history. One occurred in the years around 1600, and the other is happening right now.

History doesn't come with sharp edges, of course, but sometime around the turn of the seventeenth century there began what is often called the modern period, or modernity.[1] It lasted, roughly, until sometime in the late twentieth century. The vigorous youth of this period is often called the Enlightenment—a piece of successful propaganda if there ever was one. The Enlightenment lasted, more or less, from 1650 to 1750, but it set the tone for the centuries that followed. The modern period is defined by a distinctive worldview, forged in all its essentials during the Enlightenment, which we'll label "modernism" for lack of anything better. Before the modern period the big ideas in the air were different, and as the modern worldview overtook them, the culture changed dramatically. Some of the elements of that change, both causes and effects, include: the Scientific Revolution, including the ideas of Galileo and Newton; the declining influence of the Catholic Church in politics; the rise of nation-states out of feudal kingdoms; the slow changeover from monarchy to democracy; capitalism; and the Industrial Revolution.

It takes a long time for new ideas to permeate a culture and transform it. The Scientific Revolution began sometime in the sixteenth century, while the Industrial Revolution wasn't in full swing until the nineteenth. Nor did the mainstays of premodernity die out completely or wither overnight. For instance, the borders of modern European states were set, more or less, in the premodern era, and the Catholic Church remains the largest single religious organization in the world. So we should be cautious about imagining a terribly sharp distinction between modernity and premodernity. Still, it remains fair to say that before the Enlightenment Western civilization was much different than it was afterwards, and this new and different period is what we call modernity.

In the twentieth century, however, characteristically modern attitudes were increasingly rejected; and now, in the twenty-first century, much of the energy and creative thinking in our culture operates off postmodern assumptions. Again, this is a slow and fitful process. But if and when the mind-set of modernism fully yields to the mind-set of postmodernism, we can expect the culture to change in ways that are just as dramatic as the changes that occurred at the birth of the modern era. We are on the cusp of those changes now.

So this is the root of the various reasons to learn about postmodernism: *the culture is changing, and postmodern ideas are driving the change.* You might want to learn about postmodernism, then, just to understand the emerging world of postmodernity around you. But there are also some specifically Christian reasons to learn about postmodernism. To understand them, however, I have to make a point about churches and cultures first.

A Church and Its Culture

Note the timing of the premodern/modern/postmodern periods, and compare them to major movements in church history. The Catholic and Orthodox churches have long premodern histories (that is, histories prior to 1600). Protestant denominations formed at the dawn of the Reformation, in the 1500s—Lutheran, Anglican, and Reformed churches, for instance—retain some of the liturgy and reverence for church tradition that marks Catholicism and Orthodoxy. (The Anabaptist tradition began at about the same time, but went in a much more radical direction.) North American fundamentalist, evangelical, and charismatic churches, with less liturgical structure or dependence on tradition, have much shallower roots in the late nineteenth to mid-twentieth centuries.

What's the point? Every institution is affected by the culture in which it lives and especially the culture in which it was born. That includes my church and denomination as well as yours. The *style* of your church—how it's decorated, how long the pastor preaches and where the pastor stands while preaching, what people wear when they attend, the time you meet, the music played or sung, what instruments are used, and so on—are influenced by cultural factors, forces emanating from the contemporary culture and/or the culture of your church's past. The *practices* of your church—how much of the budget is devoted to missions, how strongly you advocate Sunday school for children and adult education for adults and what curriculum gets used in them, techniques encouraged for evangelism and apologetics and the emphasis put on them, how often you serve communion, the leadership structure of your church, and so on—are similarly influenced by cultural factors. Culture and history even mark *doctrine*—especially attitudes on divisive subjects like baptism and communion. It is no accident that as the modern period progresses, attitudes toward the Lord's Supper become increasingly "memorial" and less "sacramental."

This may be an uncomfortable thought. You may never have considered the idea that the forces of the surrounding culture, and especially the culture of past centuries, affect how you live your individual and collective Christian life. You may have thought your church ran on nothing but the Bible and common sense. Part of what will come out, as you read through this book, is that "common sense" changes: common sense is simply an inherited and unquestioned worldview. The common sense of a person influenced by postmodernism is not the common sense of a modern, and a premodern person has yet a different kind of common sense.

Not that this will be obvious to anyone. As I said, cultures are to people what water is to fish. It's hard work to notice the culture you inhabit, and especially hard work to identify your own worldview. People with a modern mind-set are mostly raised that way. They don't come with "Modern" stamped on their foreheads, and they probably don't even think of themselves as "modern" (as opposed to "postmodern"). The same goes for postmodern people: they won't necessarily think of themselves that way. A clash of worldviews, which often comes out as different intuitions about common sense, is a phenomenon that requires a keen and educated eye to perceive.

Look again at the lists of ways I claimed that culture influenced a church—style, practice, and doctrine. Ask yourself how many of those items are really dictated by the Bible. Not many, I think you'll agree. This is a good thing. God has left people free, in many areas, so that they can live and worship in ways that are familiar and comforting both for themselves and for the people they seek to reach. Now ask yourself how much of your church's life is defined by those culturally influenced items. Perhaps you'll agree with me that it's a great deal—and those lists are only a sample.

Still, you might think, whatever *quantity* of church life is affected by the culture, those things don't touch the church's *essence*. They aren't really important, are they? Well, yes and no. Consider the Amish. The Amish branch of Christianity claims to direct its life by the plain words of scripture, and yet no Christian people are more firmly guided by human tradition, a tradition begun in the seventeenth century. Are they genuine Christians? Undeniably, yes. And yet it would be pretty naïve to suggest that their lifestyle—the "inessentials" of their faith—is not an important part of the Christian life as they live it.

The ways you and I conduct our Christian lives and the churches we attend are culturally influenced, just like the lives and churches of the Amish. We, too, live by a human tradition that does not depend strictly on scripture for its authority. There's nothing wrong with that—it's unavoidable, in fact, as I hope you'll see by the end of the book. We have to make choices about how long the service will be, what songs we'll sing during it, and myriad other questions. Whatever we choose, we'll employ the common sense we've picked up from the world around us and from the church we grew up in. The difference between the influence of culture and history on the Amish, and the influence of culture and history on the life of our churches, is that our influences are less visible (to us). They are part of the fabric of our lives; they are part of church as we've always known it. We live and move in them every day.

Christian Responses to Postmodernism

Perhaps you have already put the pieces of the puzzle together. Twenty-first-century American churches have a history and an institutional culture rooted in the modern or premodern periods—the twentieth, nineteenth, or earlier centuries. Twenty-first-century America, however, is rapidly becoming a postmodern place. If this pattern doesn't change, we can expect some kind of a disconnect between churches and the surrounding postmodern culture as the twenty-first century progresses. This prospect drives the discussions about postmodernism that I mentioned at first. Will our church services still attract people? Will our evangelistic strategies or our apologetic techniques still persuade people? Will non-Christians take a different attitude toward Christianity than they have in the past?

There are, I think, three main concerns that thoughtful Christians have when they confront postmodernism, and consequently three different reasons to learn about it. Different people have emphasized different of these concerns, and one of them may appeal to you more strongly than the others, but all of them are important for Christians in the new millennium to think about.

The moral concern. Many people believe that a turn toward postmodernism will make American culture less morally centered and—a slightly different point—more hostile to Christianity than it is now. This is because postmodernism tends toward moral relativism and the rejection of all absolutes, while Christianity has historically insisted upon moral absolutes as part of its ethical teaching and doctrinal absolutes as part of its theology. A person with this concern fears for the moral tenor of American society and the place of Christianity within it; learning about postmodernism teaches him how to combat it.

The evangelistic concern. A person with this stance simply wants to reach those who do not know Christ. If adopting a more postmodern mind-set will assist the spread of the gospel without compromising its message, she'll adopt it—but she needs to understand it first. This basic theme can vary considerably: some evangelists are willing to change their church's style to reach postmodern people, some are willing to go farther and change certain practices in the church, and some go farther yet and are willing to be flexible on certain points of doctrine to reach a postmodern audience. From this point of view, learning about postmodernism helps evangelize in a postmodern culture.

The theological concern. Some Christians believe that, since postmodernism has superseded modernism, the modern worldview has in some sense failed. The ideas that drove modernity haven't cut it. This has implications for all those churches built on modern assumptions, with a modern history and a modern institutional culture: they are destined for failure too, in the brave new postmodern world. The failure is not just a failure to make postmodern converts. On this view, the church has spent four hundred years enslaved in an Egypt of modern presuppositions and consequently has forgotten much of the best of what it has to offer. The advent of postmodernism is an opportunity to rethink both the presentation and the content of the good news about Christ, to draw more deeply on the truth of the gospel by coming at it in new ways. To learn about postmodernism, then, helps us to rediscover what Christianity is all about.

The Plan of this Book

In order to address these concerns with postmodernism in a faithful and loving way rather than a smug or defensive or panic-stricken one, what Christians need is an educated grasp of the subject. Consequently, I have written this book with the primary goal of describing and explaining postmodernism to you, the reader. The book begins with a historical overview of the intellectual and cultural changes surrounding the transitions from premodernity to modernity and from modernity to postmodernity. These transitions are covered, respectively, in chapters 2 and 3. By the end of chapter 3 we are well placed to understand how postmodernism, as a general way of looking at the world, works itself out in many areas of life and thought.

The next six chapters cover various topics of central importance to the postmodern worldview: ethics, the self, language, knowledge, culture, and history. In each case I explain premodern, modern, and postmodern perspectives on the subject, though the degree of emphasis on each era varies. (The one exception is chapter 6, on language, since there the important contrast is between the twentieth century and everything before it.) By the end of chapter 9, you will have a solid working understanding of the postmodern mind-set. In the epilogue, I step back and briefly consider some larger issues: how important postmodernism is in the larger scheme of things, what the main tension between Christianity and postmodernism is, and the general attitude a Christian ought to take toward intellectual and cultural changes in the surrounding world.

Although the primary purpose of this book is to describe and explain postmodernism, a secondary goal is to offer some advice to my fellow believers about how they ought to respond to some of the challenges postmodernism presents. At the end of each of the six topical chapters, I bring the discussion home to a particular case where postmodern attitudes are most likely to affect, or raise questions for, contemporary Christians. Sometimes these comments require only a few paragraphs. In other cases, especially when traditional Christianity and postmodernism clash most clearly and forcefully, I discuss in some detail how a Christian might go about thinking through the issues.

A last comment: In various places I illustrate the differences between modern and postmodern views using stereotyped characters, and I need a way to refer to them. As we will see in the next chapter, the modern era emphasized reason at the expense of qualities like emotion and intuition, and the reason/emotion dichotomy was often thought to be embodied in the distinction between the sexes—men more rational, women more emotional—so that men were the preferred gender. In contrast, the postmodern era has seen a reaction against this tendency to exalt reason and denigrate women. So when referring to my stereotyped characters, it seemed appropriate to use "he" as the pronoun for my modern individual, and "she" for my postmodern one.

For Further Thought

1. Why are you interested in postmodernism?
2. What aspects of your church's style, practices, or doctrine are influenced by tradition? Do you think of this as a good thing, a bad thing, or neither?
3. Pick one "traditional" aspect of your church. Do some historical research, and try to find the origin of that tradition.

Premodern and Modern Minds

Postmodernism evolved out of modernism. The modern period lasted three or four centuries before slowly giving way to postmodernity, but to understand how this happened, we have to understand the contours of the modern mind. Similarly, modernism evolved out of the mind-set of the premodern period, which lasted many centuries in its own right before it suffered the strains of a new era. I should emphasize that labeling all of human history before the Enlightenment "the premodern era" vastly oversimplifies matters. For our purposes, the important part of the premodern period lies in medieval western Europe. In this chapter, we'll take a brief look at the mental and cultural world of medieval Europeans and how the modern worldview evolved out of it.

A World of Authorities

The premodern world was organized much differently than our own. The differences can largely be traced to the roles that various traditions and authorities played in premodern society.

To begin with, the political structure placed power with kings and nobles, their authority bolstered by longstanding tradition. Before the modern period in Europe, feudalism was the near-universal form of government. People were subjects of a lord, not citizens of a republic. Lesser lords owed allegiance to greater lords, and a hereditary prince or monarch sat at the top of the feudal food chain. Social position was largely fixed at birth: the son of a peasant was a peasant, and the son of a lord was a lord. In many cases, the son of a shoemaker was a shoemaker. The laws that regulated the rights and duties of each order of citizen were given by ancient tradition or established by a local lord. The central concept of democracy—that government derives its legitimacy from the consent of the governed—was virtually unknown.

The church, like the feudal society, was organized hierarchically, with the local priest answering to a bishop, and the bishop answering to the pope in Rome. Since the Roman Catholic Church enjoyed state support and the Reformation hadn't yet divided western Europe, Catholicism was the state religion from Dublin to Warsaw and from Stockholm to Naples. (Eastern Europe's allegiance was to the Orthodox Church, headquartered in Byzantium.) A few dissenters, mostly Jews, were tolerated with generally poor grace. Atheism was practically unheard of, and heresy was punishable by death, although the punishment wasn't often inflicted.

The church had many worldly powers: bishops and abbots were often powerful figures with their own feudal privileges. Tithing was mandated by law, and the funds provided by this tax supported the church. More important, however, the church was a person's connection to God. It was through baptism, the Eucharist, public prayer, and religious burial that a person expressed and experienced his religious life. Hence, the most severe penalty the church could inflict was excommunication, which meant, roughly, the denial of fellowship in Christian society. In a thoroughly Christian society, this was a grave penalty indeed.

Moreover, the religious authorities set the content of the faith—its dogmas and doctrines, and the proper interpretation of scripture. In this they depended on the Bible, reason, and the tradition of councils and church fathers. Reading the Bible was discouraged among laypeople, on the grounds that they lacked the education and proper understanding of the faith to interpret it correctly.

Traditional authorities also dominated education. University curricula centered on thorough familiarity and deep understanding of a few canonical texts, in particular the Bible, the works of the church fathers, and the writings of a few ancient pagans, especially Aristotle. The assumption behind this model of education—a model with very ancient roots—was that great authors of the distant past had worked out everything that was fundamentally important. The task of each new generation was to retrieve those truths, understand them, comment on and elucidate them, and pass them on to the next generation.

This task was undertaken in two different ways. Scholars in urban universities, beginning from traditionally authoritative texts, interpreted them using techniques of rational argument, with the aim of greater knowledge. Monks and nuns in the mostly rural monasteries and convents relied on slow, repetitive, devotional rumination over Bible passages—a process called *lectio divina,* or "divine reading"—to purify the soul and draw the reader into a deeper spirituality. These different attitudes toward education shared a fundamental confidence that what was needed for both knowledge and virtue could be found in the resources of tradition.

And that is what you could say about those who got any schooling at all. The vast majority of people lacked all education; the ability to read was rare outside clerical circles and not universal within them. For news, opinion, religious instruction, and such knowledge of history and the wider world as they could accumulate, most people depended uncritically on the say-so of others.

As a result of this confluence of feudal government, established church hierarchy, and nonexistent or tradition-oriented education, an ordinary person in the premodern period was not free in many of the senses we now recognize. He did not have any political freedom to speak of—his unelected king or lord was the undisputed ruler of the local territory, and it was difficult, if not impossible, to pick up and move. The rights we recognize as so important—freedom of the press, freedom of speech, and freedom of assembly—were absent. He did not even have freedom of conscience, since the Catholic Church was the only authorized religion and reserved for itself the right to pronounce on matters of salvation, ethics, and much else. Finally, an ordinary person was not what we would call intellectually free. Most people had very little education at all. But even those who did were given an education that emphasized not skeptical questioning or empirical experimentation, but careful study of authoritative texts. This attitude was calculated to give the student an appreciation of all the wisdom that could be found in the tradition. It was not, however, an attitude suited to uncovering errors in the received texts or in the traditional interpretation of them.

The Rejection of Authority

In the fifteenth and sixteenth centuries, this world of interlocking authorities came under increasing pressure. Any number of forces worked toward this end, and it is not always easy to say what was cause and what was effect. I'll just enumerate some of the stronger currents working to change society around the turn of the seventeenth century.

Undoubtedly one major shock to the medieval order was the Protestant Reformation. By 1550 Catholicism had lost to the Reformers huge swaths of Europe, including Switzerland, Scandinavia, Hungary, most of Germany, and some parts of France, the Netherlands, and eastern Europe. England and Scotland were to follow shortly. The Reformation was not, in general, a peaceful movement. In the struggle for territory among Lutherans, Calvinists, and Catholics, priests and bishops on both sides were frequently expelled or executed, churches were looted and burned, and adherents of one side or the other were killed. The violence culminated in the Thirty Years' War, 1618–48, which cemented the new religious divisions and prevented Germany's national unification for two centuries.

The causes of the Reformation were many and various. Protestants are most familiar with the theological disputes that preceded it, especially Luther's doctrine of *sola fide,* justification by faith alone. Probably equally important at the time, and more important for our purposes, is the doctrine of *sola Scriptura,* that is, that scripture was the sole ultimate authority for the Christian life. Who decides what scripture dictates? For the early Reformers like Luther and Calvin, it was *their* churches, as opposed to the Roman Catholic Church. Later, others claimed the right to interpret scripture for each individual believer. In any case, *sola Scriptura* is a rejection of the ecclesiastical authority of the Catholic hierarchy. Martin Luther implicitly leaned on this new doctrine in his famous defense before the pope's representatives at Worms in 1521:

Unless I am convinced by Scripture and plain reason—I do not accept the authority of the popes and councils, for they have contradicted each other—my conscience is captive to the Word of God.

Contests over the right to interpret scripture were really a way-station to modernism, halfway between the premodern and modern worlds, for under *sola Scriptura,* the Bible is still an unquestioned authority. It did not remain so as the modern period wore on. If conscientious individuals could question the church's traditional interpretations of the Bible, could they not question the claims of the Bible itself? This critical approach to all authority led to a number of variations on traditional Christianity. The idea of unitarianism, which got its name from its denial of the doctrine of the Trinity, began around the time of the Reformation and grew during the early modern period, though the Unitarian Church appeared later. Herman Reimarus's *The Goal of Jesus and His Disciples,* published posthumously in 1778, inaugurated investigations into the "historical Jesus"— that is, treatments of Jesus as a historical figure like Julius Caesar, discerned without theological commitments. The results of these critical investigations invariably conflicted with orthodox Christian teaching. Finally, deism, whose adherents included Voltaire and Thomas Jefferson, became a creed in its own right during the 1700s. Deism said that a Supreme Being had set the world in motion but had not interfered since. Deists accepted revelation only insofar as it could be reconciled with reason, which ruled out miracles, the efficacy of prayer, and many other orthodox aspects of Christianity. As an influential religious movement, deism didn't last long; historically, it was a stepping-stone on the way to atheism.

Also hammering at traditional society were intellectual forces. According to the received Aristotelian worldview, the earth sat unmoving at the center of the universe. The earth was highly imperfect, and predictable only in vague ways. The heavens, however, were orderly, harmonious, and perfect. Heavenly bodies, which were perfect spheres, moved in mathematically precise circular motions around the earth. Nicolas Copernicus began upsetting this tidy picture when in 1543 he published his major treatise, *On the Revolutions of the Celestial Orbits*. This book claimed that the center of the universe was near the sun and that the earth moved around it.

The next blow came from Galileo, who between 1610 and 1638 published various works against the Aristotelian system. He showed that the sun and moon were not perfect, incorruptible spheres: the moon had peaks and valleys, while the sun had sunspots. He observed that Jupiter had moons and that Venus went through phases, two observations that supported heliocentric astronomy. By dropping different weights off the tower of Pisa, he showed that objects of different weights fall at the same rate, something Aristotle had denied.

The Inquisition questioned Galileo and eventually sentenced him to house arrest on the grounds that his teachings contradicted scripture and church teaching. The book of Joshua claimed that the sun stood still during a battle—if the sun didn't move, how could that be? Other verses in the Psalms cited the earth's firm foundations. (Luther had earlier criticized Copernicus on much the same grounds.) As Galileo's views became more widely accepted, however, this resistance cost the church some credibility.[1]

In 1686, Isaac Newton's *Principia Mathematica* laid out a complete theory of motion for both the heavens and the earth. Whatever authority Aristotle's scientific work still had at that point was demolished completely.

This series of events had far-reaching repercussions in the world of philosophy. It is interesting to compare two thinkers separated by about fifty years, one French and the other English. René Descartes was a brilliant mathematician and philosopher. He was educated by Jesuits, and while he was grateful for his education, the shocks to its Aristotelian underpinnings were such that he felt compelled to reject it all and start again from the beginning. His *Meditations on First Philosophy* is an inquiry into basic questions of human life that in an earlier time were uncontroversial staples of Christian belief: whether God exists, whether the soul can be immortal, whether we are created in such a way as to be able to know and understand our world. Its opening sentence reads,

> Several years have now elapsed since I first became aware that I had accepted, even from my youth, many false opinions for true, and that consequently what I afterward based on such principles was highly doubtful; and from that time I was convinced of the necessity of undertaking once in my life to rid myself of all the opinions I had adopted, and of commencing anew the work of building from the foundation, if I desired to establish a firm and abiding superstructure in the sciences.

The other thinker, five decades later and on the opposite side of the English Channel, was John Locke, a scholar, political thinker, and later a government functionary. His *Essay Concerning Human Understanding,* published in 1690, is an extended investigation into what we can know and how we can know it. In the "Epistle to the Reader," which prefaces that work, he writes,

Were it fit to trouble thee with the history of this Essay, I should tell thee, that five or six friends meeting at my chamber, and discoursing on a subject very remote from this [the topic was the relation between ethics and religion], found themselves quickly at a stand, by the difficulties that rose on every side. After we had awhile puzzled ourselves, without coming any nearer a resolution of those doubts which perplexed us, it came into my thoughts that we took a wrong course; and that before we set ourselves upon inquiries of that nature, it was necessary to examine our own abilities, and see what objects our understandings were, or were not, fitted to deal with.

Locke and Descartes went on to arrive at very different views about the human mind and the proper starting points for reasoning. The commonality between Locke and Descartes, however, was the problem they faced. Descartes saw a breakdown in the old verities; he felt compelled to prove the existence of God, the independence of the soul from the body, and even the reality of the world outside his own mind, all from first principles. Locke's companions had no common source to settle disputes about ethics and religion; he resorted to an extensive and highly abstract discussion of the powers of the human mind in order to do what he could to provide some basis for agreement. Although both Descartes and Locke thought of themselves as Christians, neither felt able to appeal to revelation or to the longstanding teaching of the universal church for solace on basic questions of human life. Both thinkers resorted to the unaided powers of the natural human mind. And as it happens, both men were confident in those powers: the reasoning power of a human being, they believed, is competent to answer his deepest questions.

The political world, though perhaps a bit behind the religious or intellectual world, was also in ferment. One significant trend was an increasing emphasis on the rights of the individual. The background to this idea was that individuals are created by God, and therefore they have certain rights that cannot be removed by any created entity, such as the state. The idea that political authority derived from God was hardly new, but before 1600 or so it had been applied mostly to kings, who were alleged to hold their positions by "divine right," or to the pope, God's representative on earth. Its application to individuals was a novel step. One of the classic expressions of natural individual rights is in the American Declaration of Independence, written in 1776:

> We hold these Truths to be self-evident, that all Men are created equal, that they are endowed by their Creator with certain unalienable Rights, that among these are Life, Liberty, and the Pursuit of Happiness . . .

The theory of natural rights led logically to another theory, that the authority of a state ultimately rested with the people it governed. This, too, was a fresh idea; it undercut the whole premodern apparatus of monarchy and aristocracy. The Declaration of Independence continues,

> . . . That to secure these Rights, Governments are instituted among Men, deriving their just Powers from the Consent of the Governed, that whenever any Form of Government becomes destructive of these Ends, it is the Right of the People to alter or to abolish it, and to institute new Government, laying its Foundation on such Principles, and organizing its Powers in such Form, as to them shall seem most likely to effect their Safety and Happiness.

Note that, in exercising their right to institute new government, the people should organize it in whatever way they think best. All the main natural-rights theorists, including

Jefferson in America, Locke in England, and Jean-Jacques Rousseau in France, thought of human beings as basically rational and good. That is what gives them the ability to govern themselves. Human beings don't need political caretakers—lords or kings—they are competent to organize their own affairs.

This sentiment led naturally to a second political trend in the modern period, the increasingly efficient use of government to solve social problems. Now, government has been solving social problems since it was invented, and suggesting reforms in government in order to solve them better was no modern innovation. But in the 1700s, roughly, people began thinking beyond mere tweaks to the now-creaking medieval apparatus of society. They were inspired by Newton: if a few simple laws could explain the motions of heaven and earth, then surely the same scheme could be applied to society. Reasoning from first principles about human nature, they hoped to come up with laws that would assure, in a widely used phrase, "the greatest happiness for the greatest number." The ultimate goal was a prosperous, happy, peaceful society, constructed on the basis of a scientific understanding of humanity.

Often these laws were, in fact, vast improvements on what had gone before. The ideas of one English reformer, Jeremy Bentham, transformed the London docks from a sink of crime and fraud to a well-regulated, productive commercial site. A frequent theme in the proposed regulations was the centralization of power in a bureaucracy at the national level. Thus, for instance, by the end of the eighteenth century virtually all of France was administered from Paris. This use of nationwide bureaucracies to solve social problems is one historical origin of socialism. The planned economies of the old Communist bloc are an extreme case of attempting to manage a society by centralized bureaucracy. The United States, however, has a gentler version of the same idea: Social Security, the Patent Office, and the Postal Service are all federal bureaucracies designed to solve specific social problems.

Premodern and Modern Church Services

The history of the church has reflected the evolution from premodernism to modernism in many ways. One clear example lies in the changing structure of worship services. The services of churches with their roots in the premodern period are markedly different from the services of more recently minted denominations. The shift in emphasis from premodern tradition to modern reason is easy to see when you look closely at these different formats for worship.

In a premodern church service, for instance—the sort of service the church had for centuries and that is still followed in its main outlines by Catholic, Orthodox, Lutheran, and Anglican churches—the high point of the service is the Eucharist, which is celebrated every week. Leading up to the eucharistic celebration will be congregational singing, prayer, readings from the Bible, a short sermon, the collection of the offering, confession, and announcements, all necessary in the life of the church. For these traditions, however, the *essential* part of the Christian life lies in none of these activities. The essential thing, and the high point of the morning, is that one meets God in the wine and bread, in a ceremony as old as Christianity itself.

Of course, this premodern view only makes sense in the context of a "high" theology of communion—you can't get away with simply saying that the Lord's Supper is a way to remember Christ's death. Why have many Christians rejected this high theology, universal in the premodern church and maintained, in different ways, even by Luther and Calvin? Surely one reason—though not the only reason or even the historically original reason—is that the idea that bread becomes flesh and wine becomes blood, in any literal sense, is, to modern ears, irrational. It doesn't fit with the scientific tenor of the modern age. And if you're eating plain bread and drinking plain wine (or even plainer grape juice!), what else could the rite be but purely symbolic?

Contrast the traditional, Eucharist-centered service with the structure of the typical low-church Protestant service. The service peaks not at communion, which is celebrated comparatively rarely, but at the sermon. The sermon itself usually concentrates on drawing out some truth from one or more Bible passages. It takes the form of a lecture: the speaker talks for twenty minutes or so, without interruption, showing his audience the truths that the Bible contains. The congregation listens passively for the most part, though some people may take notes. The goal is the transmission of knowledge. Upon leaving, the members of the congregation are supposed to know something that they didn't know before, or have some truth that they already knew refreshed in their minds. Often the hope is that this new or refreshed knowledge will have practical effects in the lives of the congregation. But the practical part is an effect, and the cause is their new or refreshed knowledge. The central assumption made in structuring a service this way is that a certain kind of knowledge—the deeper understanding of the scriptures—is the key to spiritual growth. Teaching, therefore, is the main function of the church.

Thus a modern sensibility, unable to see how communion could be anything but symbolic, played a part in creating a new way of thinking about the church, one focused on teaching, or the transmission of knowledge. Consequently, that same modern sensibility also helped to create a new structure of church service, centered on the sermon. Of course, other focal points are possible. Once you cease thinking that the most important aspect of the Christian life is the grace transmitted through the body and blood of Christ in the Eucharist, you don't necessarily have to begin thinking that it's knowledge of the Bible. You could emphasize prayer, or the indwelling of the Holy Spirit, or service to others, and there are branches of Christianity that have taken all these tacks.

From Authority to Reason

I have spent so much time detailing the strains and shocks that attended the birth of the modern worldview in order to point out how much we still have invested in it, three or four hundred years later. Many of the changes enumerated above are likely to seem to us like advances. Taking political authority out of the hands of aristocrats and kings and placing it in the hands of the people is central to democratic government. Allowing science to proceed by experiment and subjecting intellectual figures to critical scrutiny are essential parts of what scholarship means these days. Putting the Bible in the hands of each person, rather than requiring people to take their cues from the priest who takes his cues from Rome, is a foundation stone of Protestant faith.

A double thread runs through all these changes. Its first strand is the rejection of some kind of traditional authority—the Roman hierarchy, the Bible, Aristotle, the king. Its second strand is replacing that trust in traditional authority with trust in individual or collective human reason, that is, trust in the natural human capacity to think things through. Every single innovation of the modern period that I have mentioned, from critical appraisals of Christianity to Social

Security, is a case of trust in the human capacity to figure out what is true and good.

Faith in the power of reason is the central pillar of the modern worldview. In the modern mind-set, every person is endowed with reason (or, more grandly, Reason). Reason might be stunted by lack of education, darkened by superstition, or cowed by the weight of tradition. But it is there, all the same, and one needs only the courage to use it. The darkness and backwardness of the Middle Ages, according to the modern way of thinking, was due to the suppression of reason in ordinary people during that time. With the encouragement and cultivation of reason, on the other hand, we can expect progress in science and society. The only obstacles are ignorance and fear, and those can be overcome with education and courage.

This is the modern worldview that postmodernism reacts against. In the next chapter, we'll see how that reaction takes shape.

For Further Thought

1. Consider the structure of political authority in the United States (or your own country). What are the underlying reasons for that structure? Contrast these with the reasons for alternative structures (for instance, monarchy, or collectivism) that other nations have employed.

2. Consider the structure of authority or governance in your church. What are the underlying reasons for that structure? Contrast these with the reasons for alternative structures (for instance, governance by elected boards of elders, or by appointed bishops) that other forms of Christianity have employed.

3. The United States has a tradition of "separation of church and state." What does this mean? Is it a good idea, or not? Why?

4. Figure out who has the authority to interpret scripture in your church. That is, who will get listened to respectfully, and who won't? What do people have to do (or be) to get this status?

The Postmodern Turn against Reason

The Faith and Hope of Modernism

The heart of the modern worldview was confidence in human powers of reasoning. With the proper use of reason, any problem—social, political, personal, or ethical—could be overcome. From faith in reason came hope in progress. If the modern worldview were right—if reason, a natural capacity for good and rational decisions, really were distributed universally, or nearly so—then you could expect things to get better and better. It wouldn't happen all at once, of course. But better science, better theology, and better government could be expected to emerge over time. This modern faith in progress is the origin of the notion that science is getting closer and closer to a true theory of everything; it is also the origin of the idea that democracy and free markets are destined to spread around the globe (as well as of the now-discredited belief in a worldwide communist revolution). Belief in progress is a corollary of modernism.

Another thing you could expect would be increasing agreement. As the use of reason weeded out more and more wrong opinions, you could expect a slow but steady meeting of minds on scientific, religious, political, and moral questions. As scientists converge on the true account of reality, you could expect a gradual diminishing of dissent on scientific questions. You could equally, and probably more importantly, expect a gradual diminishing of dissent in political matters. As the use of reason generated wiser and wiser ways of governing, solving more and more social problems, societies should become not only better but more peaceful.

These two modern predictions—gradual improvement and increasing agreement—have consequences for how a modern person thinks of cultural life. For the modern, cultures are destined to improve. Over time, the light of reason will lead people everywhere to converge on the best way of living: the most accurate science, the most powerful technology, the most beneficent political order, the highest morality, the most prosperous economy, and so on. And in fact, the major figures of the Enlightenment were cosmopolitans, looking forward to the establishment of a worldwide (or at least Europe-wide) brotherhood of humankind founded on rational principles, anticipating the dissolution of regional and ethnic differences. The modern faith in reason is, in effect, a faith that there is one right way, the rational way, to see any particular question; it is faith in the existence of One True Culture, the culture of reason. The modern hope in progress is the hope that everyone can be brought to see things the one right way and so adopt the One True Culture.

It was self-evident to moderns that Western nations were furthest along toward achieving a culture ruled by reason alone. It had far to go, no doubt, but certainly Europe was better off in this regard than the uncivilized "savages" of Africa and South America or the backward societies of Persia and China. E. B. Tylor, an early anthropologist, represented the modern attitude when he wrote,

> Civilization actually existing among mankind in different grades, we are enabled to estimate and compare it by positive examples. The educated world of Europe and America practically settles a standard by simply placing its own nations at one end of the social series and savage tribes at the other, arranging the rest of mankind between those limits according as they correspond more closely to savage or to cultured life.[1]

To the extent that they thought beyond the borders of Europe at all, modern people assumed that Europeans should, and would, export their enlightened culture to others. After all, who, having seen the benefits of reason, would refuse those benefits for himself?

The Postmodern Loss of Confidence

Premoderns placed their trust in authority. Moderns lost their confidence in authority and placed it in human reason instead. Postmoderns kept the modern distrust of authority but lost their trust in reason and have found nothing to replace it. This is the crux of all postmodern thought.

What happened? In some respects, the modern faith has panned out, and reason has delivered the goods. Scientific and technological progress are not only rapid but accelerating: we have visited the moon, and we all have DVD players. At the same time, it is hard to avoid the thought that advancing science and technology are the least important promises of modernity. The deeper aspects of life have not shown the same kind of progress. Indeed, this failure to make progress on moral and humanitarian fronts led to a triple disappointment with modern thought.

First, the modern hope in progress depended on the assumption that reason would be used in the service of humanity, or more briefly, that humans were innately good or at least were being transformed in that direction. As the nineteenth century moved on into the twentieth, this assumption looked increasingly implausible. The First World War (1914–1918) taught Europeans that even the countries most influenced by the Enlightenment could engage in tremendous amounts of pointless slaughter. During the Second World War, the Holocaust, with its enormous numbers of victims, demonstrated the bureaucratic efficiency that an evil regime could apply to genocide. And the same postwar decades that saw the invention of the polio vaccine and the eradication of smallpox also saw the development of increasingly powerful weapons of mass destruction.

Second, modernism had issued predictions that simply didn't come true. For instance, religion didn't develop the way that modernism said it would. Religion was supposed to dry up and blow away as people became increasingly rational and freed from superstition; or it was supposed to convert itself into a purely rational faith, shorn of elements due to revelation. At the very least, religious violence should have ceased, and religion become a private hobby like stamp collecting. None of this, of course, has happened.

The eventual failure of communism was another blow. Communism was a quintessentially modern project, based on Marx's "science of history" and envisioning an inevitable progress of humanity from ancient slavery through feudal agriculture, industrial capitalism, the future dictatorship of the proletariat, and culminating in "pure communism," a state of shared labor and perfect freedom. Communism was supposed to lead to a reign of peace, equality, and material comfort; it led instead to economic decline and to human rights violations on a fantastic scale.

It was not just in communist countries that the promise of modernism failed, however. Democracy and free markets, supplemented by wise government regulation, were also supposed to lead to a society of freedom and equality. But in western Europe and in the United States, social problems persisted and even increased. The government programs designed to combat these problems inaugurated the welfare state. In America, the two great phases in the growth of the welfare state were Roosevelt's New Deal of the 1930s and Johnson's Great Society programs of the 1960s. Yet, in spite of some successes, no government program has eliminated poverty, or reconciled the races, or eradicated crime, or restored the environment. Any observer can tell that the meanest motives, not the noblest, motivate much of what goes on in contemporary politics. Our statesmen are not wiser and wiser; things are not getting better and better.

Faced with these failed predictions, however, one could always argue that modernism just needed more time. Nevertheless, a growing suspicion that modernism's recipe was part of the problem rather than part of the solution—modernism *itself* was the source of moral and humanitarian failure—gradually birthed postmodernism. In broad outline, the critique goes like this: modernism, with its emphasis on reason, insists on resolving and eliminating the differences between people. But this leads, eventually, to coercion, oppression, domination, cruelty, and abuse of one form or another. Anyone who believes in One True Culture—one right way of doing things—is, knowingly or not, a closet tyrant.

Several events in the early twentieth century cemented this suspicion. By this time, European powers had colonized nearly all of Africa and a good portion of Asia. This state of affairs began to unravel by mid-century: India became independent in 1947, Kenya in 1963, Djibouti not until 1977. It was a point not lost on the colonized peoples, or on sensitive Westerners, that underneath the rhetoric of a "white man's burden," the very countries that officially preached democracy, Christianity, and the equality of all human beings had used their technological superiority to exploit the colonies' lands and labor for naked economic and military advantage.

The problem with colonialism was not merely a matter of hypocrisy. The agenda of the colonial powers, or at least its effect, had been in one way or another to erase the native cultures they colonized, on the assumption that enlightened, rational, European culture was the pinnacle toward which all others should aspire. This happened in large ways, as when African villagers were pressed into farming cash crops for a world economy instead of staples for local use. And it happened in smaller but no less important ways, as when missionaries encouraged their converts to dress in frock coats and top hats. The reaction among reflective people was that you couldn't trust the motives of the merchants of modernism. But even if you could, did you want to buy what they were selling? For it meant the end of everything special and unique about non-Western cultures.

In this milieu was born the discipline of anthropology. Anthropologists focused on the myriad ways that human cultures can form and flourish. They portrayed these cultures as valid ways of life in their own right, rather than assuming that Western culture was the model to which all other ways of life should conform. In the process, they taught Westerners to think in terms of cultures, that is, to see their own way of life as but one of many possibilities. The modern beacon of the One True Culture dimmed: why not let a thousand cultural flowers bloom?

Another seminal event in the rejection of modernism was the Holocaust. Not only was it a horrifically evil event, and not only was this great evil perpetrated with a great deal of rational calculation, but the Nazi vision was a mere variation on the modern vision of One True Culture. It was precisely the Nazis' insistence on one cultural ideal, an ideal that German Jews, communists, homosexuals, Gypsies, and others could not or would not conform to—in short, an intolerance for differences between people—that led to the horrors of Auschwitz.

Finally, the Cold War didn't reassure anybody. For several decades the two most powerful countries in the world were poised as if on a knife-edge to annihilate each other in a nuclear firestorm. It was no accident that each country considered itself the embodiment of universal ideals for humanity. People began to think that the greatest enemy of humanity was neither communism nor capitalism, but the attitude of each system that it was the destiny of mankind. Once again, it was the siren song of a single right way of life that seemed destined to lead not to universal happiness, but to universal destruction.

Postmodern Reactions

In the eyes of postmoderns, then, modernism has failed, both as a prediction of progress and as a moral framework for culture. As a result, postmoderns take distinctly anti-modern views on the deeper questions of human life: social, political, moral, and spiritual questions. The failure of modernism means that there is no universal agreement and no prospect of universal agreement on these questions. Postmoderns draw a range of conclusions.

On the optimistic side, they conclude that these fundamental questions will never be resolved through the use of reason or through appeal to an authority that already has the answer—though perhaps they can be resolved some other way. A typical optimistic postmodern hopes to *create* enough universal agreement for people to get along through teaching people to care about one another. In pressing for this expansion of fellow-feeling, she doesn't appeal to anything "already there"—our common humanity, the moral law, human rights, or whatever. No such thing dictates humanity's path. If we are to live together peaceably, that life has to be invented or constructed. We don't find it already written on our nature or in a sacred book.

Pessimistic postmoderns will agree that both reason and authority are bankrupt as ultimate guides to life. On the other hand, they generally will not put much faith in the optimist's constructive project either—perhaps the great questions of human life cannot be resolved at all. Moreover, they may also think that this unresolvability is a good thing. Unresolved differences over how to live are, in a strange way, guarantees of freedom: they ensure that we will never have anything masquerading as the One True Culture. There will always be unsuppressed differences among people.

At any rate, for a postmodern, the modern hope is dead: basically opposed parties will never work out their differences through reasoned dialogue. Reason is not a tool powerful enough to do that kind of work; it is not the universal solution that modernism thought it was. The upshot is that resolving basic questions is not a matter of having the right knowledge. Finding answers to these questions is, at minimum, not a matter of finding the truth.

Three Worldviews—a Thumbnail Sketch

In this chapter and the last I have sketched out the different ways in which premoderns, moderns, and postmoderns approach the big questions of human life, emphasizing authority or reason or, finally, our inability to find answers to these questions. Here is an oversimple but useful way to keep these three competing perspectives in order. No one can consistently believe all three of the following things:

1. Anything that's true and knowable is something people should be able to figure out and come to a consensus on.
2. There is no present consensus, and no foreseeable future consensus, on the big questions of human life—what the universe is fundamentally like, and how we should live in it.
3. The big questions of human life have answers that are true and knowable.

These three claims can't all be true. If you believe that we should be able to come to an agreement on anything true and knowable—or, put the other way around, if you believe that chronic disagreement is a sign that a bogus question is being asked (think: what's the best music of the last decade?)—and you also believe that people are not going to agree on the big questions of human life, then you believe #1 and #2. But then you should not believe #3, that the big questions have true, knowable answers. If, however, you do believe #3, and you also believe #1, that we can expect a consensus about knowable truths, then you should not believe #2, that the big questions will remain forever mired in disagreement. However, if you believe #2, and also believe #3, that there are nevertheless answers to these questions, then you should not believe #1.

As I said, these three claims can't all be true. The problem is, there is something to be said for each of them. In favor of #1, we have it deeply ingrained in us that a normal adult can understand and come to believe anything that has a good argument behind it; chronic disagreement (on, say, nutritional advice, or the remedy for poverty in developing nations) is usually a sign that people don't really know what they're talking about. In favor of #2, we have the empirical evidence of history and our own deeply divided American politics. And giving up #3 seems like a capitulation to hopelessness—what is left for figuring out how to live your life?

As you may have guessed, people with different mindsets respond differently to this conundrum. The premodern mind is not impressed with #1. The premodern conception of moral, political, and spiritual knowledge is much less "democratic" than ours—a premodern assumes that such knowledge requires either being an expert or listening to an expert. There is no more likelihood that the man in the street will come up with a proper life ethic on his own than that he will come up with a proper theory of quantum physics on his own.

The modern mind refuses to accept #2. Moderns believe in progress: while there may be no consensus today on difficult questions of morality and society, we have some good ideas—liberal democracy, market capitalism underwritten by a social safety net, universal education, maximum personal freedom—and we can expect increasingly better ideas, accepted more widely, as time goes on.

The postmodern takes the final option, rejecting #3. The big questions of life have no definitive answers. Or if they do, they elude us systematically, and our grasp of them is necessarily dim. She may or may not think that a community can create some provisional attempt at a good life for its members, for instance, by teaching them to be kind and thoughtful. But any such arrangement will no doubt be flawed, subject to revision, requiring yet more tinkering in the future, with no final rest expected.

Postmodern Options

I have described postmodernism as a certain loss of faith—faith in the power of reason to resolve differences and deliver solutions—and a consequent loss of hope—hope in progress based on human knowledge. Very few post-moderns would stop there, however. Postmodernism takes many different forms, but these variants can all usefully be seen as attempts to explain the inability of reason to resolve fundamental questions of human life.

There is, for instance, *nihilism,* which says that we cannot resolve basic questions because there simply is no right answer. Or a postmodern might advocate *relativism* in either its radical or cultural guises: relativism is the idea that truth varies from person to person (radical relativism), or from society to society (cultural relativism). A variation on this, one that is very common among postmoderns, is *constructivism,* which says that basic questions cannot be resolved because truth is made, or constructed, rather than discovered. Different people or different societies construct different truths; hence, their truths are different, so of course not everyone is going to agree on them. Or there is *pragmatism,* which says that truth is just whatever helps us get around in life. Whether you are getting around in life, however, depends in part on what you aim to accomplish, so truth will differ between people or between cultures that aim to accomplish different things.

Here we can point out some common misconceptions about postmodernism. Relatively few postmoderns reject the notion of *truth* entirely. Relativists, constructivists, and some pragmatists all allow for certain kinds of truth. They do, however, reject the idea of *absolute* truth, that is, truth that doesn't vary among cultures, or people, or fundamental goals in life. Yet even in rejecting absolute truth, they don't have to reject it for everything. For instance, many postmoderns will allow that a fact like, "Rhode Island is the smallest state in the U.S." is a perfectly absolute truth. It's the larger questions of human life—moral, social, and political claims; claims about how we should live—that postmoderns definitively refuse to think of as having absolute answers.

The denial of absolute moral truth, one of postmodernism's hallmarks, is also one of its most upsetting characteristics for many people, Christian or not. To anyone of a traditional cast of mind, the end of absolute moral truth is the end of ethics—anything goes! The next chapter is devoted to understanding this aspect of postmodernism, and in particular, to understanding some of the distinctly *ethical* concerns that drive postmoderns to deny absolute truths of morality.

For Further Thought

1. The world is not the best place it could be. In your view, why not? What is needed to make it better? How would some of your friends answer this question?
2. Do you think scientific advances are generally a good thing? Why?
3. Describe what you think life will be like two hundred years from now.

4. Compare the following statements:

—"Rhode Island is the smallest state in the U.S."
—"God exists."
—"Murder is wrong."
—"Peanut butter and jelly sandwiches are delicious."

Is one statement "truer" than another? What is meant by "truer" here?

Truth, Power, and Morality

The modern mind-set has been characterized by a search for truth and a confidence that it would be found. It expected the science of nature to come up with a definitive account of the universe and everything in it, and it expected the science of human conduct to arrive at a similarly definitive account of how people ought to live. By this yardstick, natural science is arguably doing okay; it hasn't yet arrived at the grand theory of everything, but it looks like it's making progress. (Not that all postmoderns or even all scientists would agree, but we'll leave that aside.) The project of coming up with a universal ethic is on much shakier ground. Postmoderns have rejected it entirely by denying any moral absolutes—any claims about how we ought to live that apply universally to all times and places and cultures and people.

This relativism presents perhaps the most contentious point between modern and postmodern worldviews. Other postmodern opinions can just seem odd, but we can live with oddity. Relativistic morality, on the other hand, has clear practical consequences. It looks like an anti-ethic that licenses any kind of vice. And yet, as we will see, this rejection of moral absolutes, which moderns (and premoderns) find so dangerous, really springs from a serious ethical concern.

My first goal, as always, is to help you understand the postmodern mind. After that, I offer some thoughts on how a Christian might respond.

Truth and Power

Whether a postmodern person identifies herself as a nihilist, relativist, constructivist, pragmatist, or something else—or simply doesn't think about it, which is not too uncommon—she also has a deeper motivation for rejecting the idea that solving basic questions of human life means finding out *the* truth about them. Her motivation can be summed up in the postmodern slogan, "Truth is power."

To see where the postmodern person who says this is coming from, consider science, the most respected source of truth in the modern world. We say that science has established certain truths. For instance, virtually everyone nowadays believes that the earth is round, and virtually everyone believes this, in one way or another, on the basis of a scientist's say-so. We've seen pictures of a round earth, or read it in textbooks, or were told it by our teachers, but these are all forms of taking someone else's word for it. It is possible to prove that the earth is round by seeing it for yourself from space or by measuring the angle of the sun on the horizon from different points at the same time, but nobody bothers to do this. We listen to the scientists.

This reliance seems entirely unremarkable. Yet it points to a kind of power that the scientific establishment has been granted in our society. For if you disagree with the scientific establishment and insist that the earth is flat or hollow or cylindrical, it won't be a matter of polite dissent. You will be treated as a wacko by scientists and everyone else. In short, on certain questions, science has the power to determine the truth, and hence the power to determine who counts as a person worth paying attention to.

This power that science wields is a form of authority. What scientists say about matters like the shape of the earth goes—not because scientists can change the earth's shape, but because they (presumably) have the tools and expertise to figure it out. But this authority has social ramifications, since anyone who bucks their authority is regarded as outside the pale of reasonable discussion. And this social consequence, in turn, is an ethical issue, for it is a grave matter to decide that someone's opinion is not worth discussing. This, then, is the meaning of "truth is power": *the authority to determine what counts as true is also the power to determine who counts as important.*

Scientific authority and power, like any authority or power, can be abused. Any Christian who has disputed an atheist's account of the evolution of life on earth will have felt it. And much worse has been perpetrated in the name of science: it was once considered a scientific "truth" that humanity was divided into dozens of races, the most evolved of which was the Nordic or Aryan northern European race; and this alleged "truth" has supported all sorts of racism from Jim Crow to the Nazis.

What goes for science—the modern paradigm of knowledge—will go for any other authority we acknowledge. In particular, it will go for any *moral* authorities we acknowledge, anyone we let tell us how we ought to live. And here the ethical stakes are much higher. For a moral authority will have the power to determine who counts as living a good life, and who a bad life; who ought to be punished, who praised; and what the limits of acceptable behavior are. Abused moral authority is much worse than abused scientific authority: we have only to consider Afghanistan under the Taliban, or the bloodletting of the Crusades, or the burning of the Salem witches, to see how far wrong it can go.

Postmodernism comes after the most violent century in history, and it carries an ethical impulse. In Africa and Asia and South America it has seen the exploitation of black and brown people in the name of the white man's burden; in the United States it has seen the mistreatment and exclusion of minorities in the name of social cohesion; in Germany it has seen genocide in the name of national destiny; in the Soviet Union, China, and Cambodia it has seen mass murder in the name of political ideology; it has seen multiple wars fought in the name of religion. Postmodernism diagnoses each of these great sins as the oppression of one group by another (which is pretty obvious), but furthermore, as oppression encouraged by some universal moral or social or political guide: "We have a duty to civilize the backward tribes." "The races must not mix." "We must eliminate the bourgeoisie in order for the dictatorship of the proletariat to commence." "The Germans ought to rule Europe; the Jews ought to be eliminated."

In the broad sense, these are all suggested moral absolutes, directions for living. It is these convictions and others like them, postmoderns feel, that have caused such misery. Because someone believed in a moral theory or a national destiny or a political program—a big picture about how everyone everywhere ought to live—they felt free to destroy or denigrate other human beings who opposed that vision.

We say, "never again," but how do we make sure such things never happen again? Postmoderns trace the problem to corrupted moral authority—the abuse of the power to say who counts and who doesn't. But, they continue, *any* moral authority is likely to have the same effect: all ways of saying who counts and who doesn't, who's wrong and who's right, who's in and who's out, are going to discriminate against someone, namely the non-counting, in-the-wrong, outside-the-pale folks. The only solution is to refuse to grant anyone moral authority: *no one* is to have the power to say how everyone should live. This amounts to denying the possibility of absolute truth about the big questions. Nihilism, relativism, and the rest are various ways of doing that.

Skeptical Postmodernism

Some postmodern authors pursue a slightly different line of thought, and it is worth exploring it in a little more detail here. Their position is basically skeptical: while they agree that some ultimate moral truth exists, they have a very low opinion of our capacity to grasp that truth and apply it to our own situations.

As an example, consider a middle-school student who gets in a scuffle in the hallway. He's hauled to the principal's office. The student claims that he was just defending himself. The principal believes him, since she knows that he has been chronically bullied and that the other student in the scuffle is a known troublemaker. On the other hand, there is a school rule against any kind of fighting, and the standard punishment is suspension. What to do? Where does justice—moral truth—lie?

Three different kinds of responses seem inadequate. The first is simply a wooden, unthinking application of the rule ("no fighting; punishment by suspension") to the case. Surely the details of the situation—the repeated abuse suffered by the student, the failure of the school to remedy it earlier—make a difference in determining the correct punishment. But it's hard to say just how much difference these factors should make, or whether the standard punishment is a just one in the first place. Any decision seems somewhat arbitrary.

The second inadequate response is paralysis. Faced with the fact that any decision seems arbitrary, and yet also faced with the necessity to do the right thing, the principal might refuse to make any decision. But that refusal, of course, would quickly lead to chaos.

The third inadequate response—inadequate from the standpoint of one who cares about moral truth—is for the principal simply to make an arbitrary decision in order to preserve school order, without caring very much whether she has done justice to the student before her. So again, what to do?

A responsible administrator has to dish out some punishment. A skeptical postmodern would insist, however, that a morally sensitive principal can neither simply ignore the details of the situation before her by applying a one-size-fits-all rule, nor feel especially confident in whatever carefully weighed decision she does make. According to this kind of postmodern view, there *is* a moral order, an ideal of justice, that the principal has to try to meet. That ideal, however, is so distant, so imperfectly discerned, that the actual real-world decision being made scarcely approaches it. The actual standards we use to make decisions—whether they be general rules like "fighting in school will be punished by suspension" or more nuanced individual decisions—can only be very imperfect approximations to the ideal.

What goes for a schoolboy in front of the principal also goes for a criminal before a judge, a disobedient child before her mother, or a rogue nation facing censure by the United

Nations. In each case, a skeptical postmodern might grant that there is justice to be done, moral truth to be upheld. She will also maintain, though, that what justice or morality amounts to in a given case is difficult or impossible to know. Are there moral absolutes? Sure. But what are they? And how do they apply at present? Here there are no firm answers, and any answer we offer is subject to revision and correction in light of better understanding.

The skeptical postmodern will say that any attitude more ambitious than hers confuses *moral absolutes* with *our conceptions of moral absolutes*. Refusing to revise or correct one's understanding of moral truth leads to an undesirable self-satisfaction in ethical matters.

For a Christian, there is a lot to admire in this line of thought, which emphasizes humility before transcendent truth. On the other hand, at a practical level, skeptical postmodernism is ambiguous. If it just amounts to an exhortation to do our best when making ethical decisions and not to be too smug about them, then really, who could object to that? Usually, however, the attitude is used to justify well-trodden postmodern paths: we ought to doubt our and others' ability to know right and wrong, and thus no one and nothing is to be granted moral authority.

The Nifty Logic Trick

For traditional Christians, the refusal to believe in moral absolutes is perhaps the most distressing aspect of postmodernism. The distress lies at the heart of what I called "the moral concern" with postmodernism in the first chapter. How should a Christian respond?

There is one popular response that I think is unhelpful. It is basically the claim that postmodernism (or more accurately, postmodernism's opposition to moral absolutes) refutes itself. I call it the Nifty Logic Trick. There are variations, but basically the argument goes like this:

> You postmodern people think that there are no moral absolutes. Well, here's a very important moral proposition:
>
> There are no moral absolutes.
>
> Is that an absolute or not? If it is, then you have contradicted yourself. If it isn't, then why should I bother with it? For my view, namely, that there are some moral absolutes, would then be just as good as yours, on your own account. So either way, your view is refuted.

As a piece of logic this argument has some merits. But it will not convince a postmodern for two reasons. First, a postmodern can always give up the logical principles on which the argument depends before giving up her opinion. Second, and much more important, no one ever gives up a cherished viewpoint unless presented with something better, and the Nifty Logic Trick fails to do that. "There are some moral absolutes" is not a worldview; it is a fragment of a blueprint for a worldview. The Nifty Logic Trick doesn't tell us what the moral absolutes are, and if we accept it as an argument, we then have to go find our missing absolutes. Probably we will have to use our reason, if we want to be moral philosophers, or appeal to a traditional authority like the Bible, if we are Christians. If the postmodern person is convinced of one thing, it is that such a search will be fruitless (in the best case) or result in something oppressive to someone (in a worse case). In any case, she is not likely to go along. Facing a choice between logical inconsistency and abetting cruelty (however well-intentioned), she chooses to be inconsistent. Only a modern could fault her.

A Christian Response—Ordering Our Own House

Christians ought to be troubled by the postmodern rejection of moral absolutes. But in responding, the first task is to get our own house in order. First of all, why are moral absolutes so important? And second, which ones are we prepared to insist upon? Full replies to these questions would take us too far off the main subject of this book, and anyway I am not sure I have complete answers. But here are some things to think about.

There are several traditional reasons to insist on moral absolutes. I won't go through all the arguments here, but the good ones boil down to an insistence that the surest way to hurt people in the long run is to abandon all moral absolutes—that these uncrossable lines are, somehow, the safeguard of every human being. The modern notion of individual human rights embodies the same idea, and has the same effect: if everyone has inalienable rights to life, liberty, and the pursuit of happiness, then it is wrong, always and everywhere and for anyone, to intentionally take away a person's life or liberty, or to frustrate their pursuit of happiness. The general idea of universal moral norms is ancient, widespread, and endorsed by practically every moral authority up until late in the modern period. Christians should not feel uncomfortable standing by it, even as they do so humbly and carefully. The danger, of course, is of tying up unnecessary burdens for others and not helping to lift them.

At the same time, on the second question—which moral absolutes to insist upon—many Christians have been guilty of very muddled thinking. One tendency is to think that the Bible contains a pretty clear list of commands, and those are the ones we should maintain. However, the Bible contains *a lot* of commands, and it requires some fairly sophisticated interpretation to evaluate them. Christians have frequently ignored some commands that are in the Bible, such as Paul's command for women to pray with their heads covered.[1] We also are somewhat more permissive about divorce and remarriage than the Bible seems to allow. On the other side, Christians have insisted on rules that are not in the Bible. For instance, historically, the church has taught that lying is always wrong. At least to my knowledge, scripture never says this. There is a long tradition opposing contraception, too, which the Catholic Church still maintains, but which, in my view anyway, is not supported in scripture. Nor does the Bible contain the prohibitions against dancing, drinking, smoking, and gambling that have played such a large role among fundamentalists. In short, the actual moral judgments of Christian communities do not support the idea that moral absolutes can be read off easily from the pages of the Bible.

A Christian Response—Defending Moral Absolutes

With those points made, I return to a different question. How should a Christian respond to the postmodern encouragements *against* moral absolutes? We have seen two lines of thought leading postmoderns to reject absolute, universal answers to questions about how to live. The first is the failure of the Enlightenment project: the progress, agreement, and cultural unity that it promised have not panned out. If there were absolute, universal rules about how to live, the thought goes, we would have found them by now. But we haven't, so there aren't. For this argument to be any good, the modern notion of the self has to be more or less accurate: we have to be rational, so that we can find the truth, and good, so that we will live it. But

Christians have no stake in this conception of the self. The doctrine of original sin tells us that the effects of sin impair both our minds and our wills. We are born in both intellectual and moral darkness. We need the influence of the Holy Spirit—in the life of Jesus Christ, in the Bible, in the historical church, and in our own consciences—to enlighten us. Since modernity rejected all these things, it's no wonder that it abounded in as much evil and discord as it has.

The second postmodern line of thought is, fundamentally, an ethical concern itself, and it deserves careful handling because it is ultimately an issue of the heart rather than the head. In essence, the postmodern argument is that the surest way to hurt people in the long run is to insist on moral absolutes—that is, precisely the opposite line from the basic argument *for* moral absolutes. Now, some people who take this line will wield it in a "your rules don't apply to me" kind of way, simply as an excuse for their own behavior. Their problem is fundamentally a matter of the will, not of the intellect. You can present them with arguments like the Nifty Logic Trick, or even much better arguments, but arguments are not likely to change their attitude. The real work begins when you confront someone who really believes that insisting on moral absolutes leads to great evils and who seeks to live by this belief out of a sense of moral conviction. The skeptical postmodern, who believes that our very ignorance of true morality is the best reason not to insist on it very strongly, holds a particularly important form of this attitude.

This moral sensibility has to be honored, and it can be appealed to. You might bring up cases where moral absolutes have been deployed, to seemingly good effect, in the face of cultural difference. For instance, when the British controlled India, they prohibited the Hindu practice of *suttee,* which involved burning a (living) widow on the same pyre with her deceased husband. The moral absolute involved is "No killing innocent people." Was it really wrong for the British to end *suttee*? Is there any real doubt about the right decision in this case? Another case is the South African divestment—the refusal of many nations to engage in economic relations with South Africa as long as the apartheid regime remained. This was a coercive action undertaken on moral grounds; the moral absolute involved is "Racial discrimination is wrong." Was it really misguided?

You can also mention precisely the great evils that have led postmoderns to reject moral absolutes: colonial exploitation, the Holocaust, totalitarian governments. Wouldn't each of these have been prevented if some tried-and-true moral absolutes had been followed? And isn't a lively respect for those very absolutes the surest way to guarantee that such enormous wrongs never happen again?

These sorts of cases, however, like the Nifty Logic Trick, may leave the postmodern relativist more frustrated than convinced. Just because she doesn't know what to say doesn't mean she'll agree with you. Here it can be helpful to point out Jesus's summary of the law: love God, and love your neighbor as yourself. At least the second part of this may very well appeal to a postmodern; it embodies the respect for others she tries to uphold. What she will doubt is that anything more concrete (no murder, no adultery, no stealing, etc.) can be derived from such an abstract principle. It then falls to you to show how a given moral rule really does express love, even if it's sometimes tough love.

An Example: Homosexuality

If you find yourself defending moral absolutes, I cannot overemphasize the importance of a truly loving attitude, a genuine concern for everyone involved. One area where

Christians might take a lesson on this is homosexuality. Conservative attitudes toward homosexuality are losing ground in our society: Canada has approved marriages between gays, some states are headed in the same direction, and laws against sodomy have been ruled unconstitutional. In trying to formulate a response, Christians often turn to the Bible and to their favorite preachers and psychologists. One set of voices rarely taken into account is that of homosexuals themselves. The honest reason is that, since homosexuals perpetrate the very sin that conservative Christians are trying to combat, what homosexuals have to say is not thought very important. Gays and lesbians are to be corrected or at least suppressed, not listened to.

This is precisely the pattern that postmodernism predicts for moral absolutes. The relevant moral rule is "Homosexual sex is wrong." A postmodern anticipates that anyone who lives by this rule will stop treating the people on the wrong side of it—in this case, gays and lesbians—as worth listening to, as really deserving of consideration. The way that much Christian discussion of homosexuality goes bears out their fears.

And yet, you might think, why should a Bible-believing Christian listen to what a homosexual has to say? Is there anything to learn from such an encounter? Perhaps. It is easy for some Christians, having little contact with gay people, to believe falsehoods about them: that homosexual relationships are always built on lust and never on love, for instance. Or that gay people don't commit to lifelong relationships. Or that they have no desire to raise families. Each of these untruths casts homosexuals as less "human" and thus less deserving of respect—less loving, less faithful to promises, more self-interested and sex-obsessed than heterosexual people. The best way to counteract such misconceptions is to listen to homosexuals themselves.

I have no special insight into how Christians ought to reply to the challenge that homosexuality represents, and faithful people have suggested widely different responses. I do know that many Christians find it easiest to circle wagons around their church's culture, talk vaguely about "traditional values," and never fundamentally engage those who disagree with them. This is the response postmoderns predict and deplore. The postmodern solution, on the other hand, is some version of hands-off relativism. Neither of these responses deals creditably with the emotional complexity, social ramifications, and sacramental mystery of sex in human life. Can we do better?

For Further Thought

1. Most of us are willing to take a geologist's word for it that the earth has tectonic plates, or an astronomer's word for it that the sun is 93 million miles away, but we are unwilling to take a politician's word for it that taxes should be raised—we want argument and proof and evidence, even if we wind up agreeing. Why do we treat politicians and scientists so differently? Why isn't politics a form of knowledge you could have expertise in, like geology or astronomy?

2. Think about the Nifty Logic Trick. Does it show what it tries to? How exactly might a postmodern respond to it?

3. Do you think there are any moral absolutes—rules that should never be broken by anyone for any reason? What are they?

4. What, in your opinion, is the most powerful argument *against* the existence of moral absolutes?

The Self

Postmodernism draws the most ire, probably, for its views on truth and morality. As we have seen, however, these controversial views stem from deeper convictions about the failure of reason (or anything else) to provide a reliable guide for life. This general worldview has broad implications. In the next several chapters, I'll examine some ways in which postmodernism departs from modern-style common sense. In this chapter I'll talk about the self.

The Self

What is "the self"? It's what defines you; it's what makes you the person you are. Answering this question with any more precision, as we shall see, depends on your worldview. Are you, fundamentally, a pleasure-seeking animal? An image of God? A rational mind? A swirling site of unresolved sexual tensions? A consumer? A collection of genes seeking to replicate themselves? A predictable product of your society? All of these answers, and many more, have been offered to questions about the self.

Inquiry into the self has a long history. Probably the first in-depth account of the self is in Plato's *Republic,* written around 370 B.C. In the premodern period, many philosophers had something to say about what makes us the way we are. In the late nineteenth century, psychology ("the study of the soul") broke off from philosophy as a distinct discipline, and the psychological theories of the twentieth century have most recently shaped reflection on the self. For instance, there is Sigmund Freud's Id/Ego/Superego construction and Abraham Maslow's theory of a hierarchy of needs.

Premoderns, moderns, and postmoderns differ dramatically in the way they think about the self. Their differences over the self reflect their differences over the source of a guide to life: an already-given tradition, human reason, or nothing at all.

The Premodern Self: Human Nature

What determines the person you are? The premodern mind thought of human beings as having a *human nature*—some set of qualities that were intrinsic and special to human beings. For example, Christianity has historically claimed that human nature consists in bearing the image of God. Followers of Augustine, and there have been many, would add that human nature includes a distortion of that image by original sin. Christians differ widely over how to understand those two doctrines, but any way they are interpreted involves some fixed characteristics shared universally by every human being.

Premodern thought allows that the characteristics given to us by our human nature (whatever we take those to be) can be covered over by socialization or other extraneous factors. For instance, the idea of creation in God's image is sometimes thought to mean that human beings have an intrinsic desire for relationship with God. As Augustine wrote, "Our hearts are restless until they find their rest in You." Now, Augustine would allow that not every pagan *feels* restless all the time. The restlessness is there, but it can be buried or dormant; one task of the evangelist is to awaken the desire for God that is at least latent in every human heart.

This distinction between what is *really* there and what only seems to be there (or seems not to be there) leads to the idea of a "true self" or a "core self." The true self, for the premodern, is what is given by human nature; it involves a human's destiny, what a person was made for. The various accretions to your personality piled on by family, society, or education are inessential additions, not really part of the self.

The idea of a human nature—an unchanging true self at the core of every human being—thus results in a certain kind of moral constraint. You aren't really free to make your life any way you want if you have a human nature; you owe it to your true self to make your life in some particular way, for instance, to find your rest in God. From a modern perspective, "human nature" is one more constraint on freedom, one more authority figure telling us how our lives ought to go. From a postmodern perspective, those who try to tell us about our human nature are pushing one more power agenda.

Modernity, in a weak way, and postmodernity, in a strong way, eventually reject the old idea of human nature. But this premodern notion is hardly dead even now. Many twentieth-century psychological theories of the self invoke the idea of a human nature in one way or another. For example, Freud thought it an inalienable part of the human condition that infant boys are in love with their mothers.

More recently, evolutionary psychologists have theorized that natural selection gives us traits like an aversion to incest or affection for kin.

Perhaps of more interest, the philosophical chestnut, "What is the meaning of life?" is a question that asks about one's true self. Someone who asks this question betrays a premodern instinct: he *wants* a pre-arranged scheme to fit into, some kind of authority to tell him what he was made for. Postmodern answers like "There isn't one," or "Life is what you make it," only satisfy those who have abandoned a premodern mind-set.

The Autonomous Modern Self

The modern mind-set picks up on a theme from the ancient Greeks, that the hallmark of the human species is reason. For the moderns, reason, shared by all human beings, though dormant or clouded in some, becomes the new human nature. In some respects, the modern exaltation of reason is simply a specific view about the human nature we have, namely, one that consists in having reason. In other respects, however, the modern story about reason is a little different from a traditional story about human nature.

Among other things, reason is the gatekeeper to the mind. At least potentially, reason allows a person to control his thoughts, beliefs, feelings, and intentions by evaluating each one, keeping and pursuing those that are rational, and rejecting those that are irrational. Thus, the man of reason determines what makes up his self and therefore controls who he is. This ideal of self-control goes by the name "autonomy." An autonomous individual is *independent*, not subject to the influences of others—unless, of

autonomous self:
human perfection

course, they are influences his reason can approve of. He is also *stable*—he does not change with whims, fashions, or opinions. This stable, independent, autonomous self is modernism's ideal.

MA – PH *autonomous self*

Benjamin Franklin's *Autobiography* gives us a fascinating picture of someone striving after this ideal. "It was about this time," he writes, meaning about 1730, "I conceived the bold and arduous project of arriving at moral perfection." There follows a list of thirteen virtues—temperance, silence, order, resolution, frugality, industry, sincerity, justice, moderation, cleanliness, tranquility, chastity, humility—that Franklin has settled on for himself and that he aims to inculcate, one by one, by deliberate practice. Published a century later in 1838, Ralph Waldo Emerson's famous essay "Self-Reliance" puts a more inner-directed spin on the same general idea. "Whoso would be a man, must be a non-conformist. . . . Nothing is at last sacred but the integrity of your own mind."

As I already mentioned, the modern perspective allows that some, even most, people do not live according to perfect reason. The autonomous exercise of reason is suppressed by the heavy hand of authority in church, state, or university and stunted by the weight of tradition or social conformity. It requires education and courage to get a populace to use their reason rather than look to inherited models for wisdom.

Nevertheless, the life according to reason is possible and desirable. Moreover, such a life—and only such a life—is truly free. The autonomous person creates himself, makes himself what he is, and runs his own life according to his own lights. His core self is not something he is merely born with, an accident of the species, but is determined by himself alone.

The Disappearing Postmodern Self

When trust in reason begins to crumble, the vision of
the autonomous modern self begins to blur. It is reason
that guards the modern mind, policing its contents, determining what will make up the self. It is reason that grants
the modern self the independence and stability that lead
to autonomy. It is reason that ensures that the modern
individual is a self-creator. But what happens when you
lose faith in reason?

I can begin by putting the question this way: how does the
modern person know what is "reasonable" and "rational,"
and what "unreasonable" and "irrational"? Thus, how
does he know which among his many possible thoughts
and feelings to absorb and which to reject? The modern
has to reply that this knowledge is innate, or easily learned.
He must have great confidence in his powers of reason,
which are unaffected by time or circumstance and are shared
universally.

The postmodern has no such confidence. We human beings are too weak, she thinks, to have the mental superpow-
ers modernism alleges. Any opinions one might have about
what is reasonable or unreasonable, rational or irrational,
are products of our culture, our family upbringing, the education we have received, and the books we read. Moreover,
she is not sure that there is a distinction between "rational"
and "irrational" elements of the self, at least, not one that
is wholly independent of history or culture, any more than
there is a transhistorical, transcultural distinction between
fashionable and unfashionable clothing.

She can doubt further. The modern's "rational absolutes," like the premodern's human nature, have all the same
problems as moral absolutes (and indeed, for the modern,
these will be the same thing): they look suspiciously like

masks for a power agenda. Whereas for moderns and pre-moderns the central fact about human beings is what they have in common, for postmoderns that central fact is the variations and differences among human beings. Emphasizing the common—the alleged human nature, or the faculty of reason—is another way of suppressing differences. Or put another way, essence is power just like truth is power: if you have the authority to say what's essential to being human, you have the power to determine who rates and who doesn't, who has lived up to the standard and who hasn't. To undercut that power, postmoderns insist that there is *no* essence to being human; that there is no human nature, only human history; that reason is influenced by culture more than the other way around.

The postmodern can't trace the self to human nature or reason. What then determines the person you are? Postmodernism views selves, not as having an intrinsic nature or as autonomous and self-controlled, but as *socially constructed*. That is, the self is put together, and made what it is, by social forces larger than any single individual. Some of this is obvious: the clothes you like to wear, the way you style your hair, even your sense of humor are largely products of the time and place in which you live as well as the social and economic strata you inhabit. Postmodernism goes further, however: your political opinions, your ethical convictions, and your religious commitments—the deepest aspects of your personality—are all shaped by parents, friends, community, the public mood during your formative years, prominent institutions like political parties or church denominations, the mass media, the economic structure of your society, and many other forces beyond your influence or ken. A more subtle, but for postmoderns very important influence on the self is the language you are taught to speak, something that will be treated in more depth in the next chapter.

Faced with socially constructed selves, again postmoderns divide into optimists and pessimists. Optimists view the infinite malleability of the self as an opportunity for emancipation, not only for oneself but for oppressed people everywhere. Social structures can change. If and when they do, attitudes change, cultures change, and therefore people (quite literally) change. Postmoderns have taken over from moderns the idea that the key to freedom is the removal of authorities of all kinds, including those would-be authoritative voices that tell us what's essential to being human, what's rational, what's natural. The key is to mobilize enough people to change a society. With enough strength, you can change what is considered normal, natural, or rational.

This is the clue to the "identity politics" that has exploded since the 1970s—the phenomenon of African Americans, Hispanics, women, gays, and others beginning to think of themselves as an aggrieved group. In many ways, these new political coalitions are inspired by Marxism. In Marx, wealth is the only power, and people are divided between capitalists, who have wealth, and workers, who don't. Consequently, the battle for power is between capitalists and workers, rich and poor; and class struggle—mobilizing the poor workers against the rich capitalists—is the logical political consequence. Since the 1970s, postmoderns have discerned many more power relationships in society than simply the haves and have-nots: men have power over women (hence feminism); whites have power over minorities (hence racial politics); straights have power over homosexuals (hence gay and lesbian political activism). Identity politics is a challenge to the claims about human nature or reason that reinforce these differences in social power:

"Men are naturally in authority over women," "Whites are superior (intellectually or otherwise) to blacks," "Homosexuality is unnatural."

Pessimistic postmoderns, however, are convinced that they ultimately have no control whatsoever over their selves. The power of outside forces is too great. Ultimately, it is the society that shapes the individual, not the individual that shapes society. Moreover, the social forces that have such power over individuals are not in general trustworthy. After all, how many of them have your best interests at heart? Madison Avenue, in particular, spends billions of dollars every year on an army of psychological experts whose sole aim is to implant desires that you otherwise would not have.

Here's an example of how well it can work. Engagement rings have been around a long time, and diamonds have been popular stones for engagement rings since at least the late Middle Ages among the well-to-do. However, in America today, many young women eagerly expect a diamond engagement ring from their fiancés, and many potential grooms anticipate buying one. This was not the situation before the 1940s. The origins of our diamond obsession can be traced directly to an advertising campaign begun in 1939, and paid for by the diamond monopoly DeBeers, in order to prop up demand for diamonds. To give you some idea of how well the strategy worked, consider that there are about two and a half million weddings every year in the United States, and that most diamond rings cost over $1000. Though no one keeps precise statistics on engagement ring revenue, a conservative estimate would put it at a billion dollars every year, a hefty portion of which makes its way back to the DeBeers company.

It's not really the money that's important, though. After all, Americans spend a lot more money than that on car repairs every year, but car repairs wouldn't make the point. The point is that wanting a diamond ring is, on the one hand, a desire with deep emotional force, and on the other, obviously socially constructed by large corporations for purposes that have nothing to do with marital happiness. DeBeers' advertisers have altered not just the purchases but the very selves of young women.

There's no need to pick on young women, though. Desires for a Jaguar, a vacation home, or a senior management position are just as obviously social constructions, even if we can't pinpoint their causes as precisely. No one would have these desires had he been raised, say, as a peasant in thirteenth-century China.

For pessimistic postmoderns, the whole self is that desire for a diamond ring writ large—all your expectations, beliefs, dreams, and desires result from forces beyond your control. Ultimately, what the moderns called "reason" is one more socially constructed disposition. Nor is there any bottoming out in human nature for a postmodern; it's social conditioning all the way down. Consequently, there is no such thing as a "core self" or a "true you." Some desires or beliefs may be harder to change than others, but given the right social conditions, any part of your self, no matter how deep, can be altered.

If this sounds cynical or frightening, you aren't the only one to think so. The postmodern envisions a human being neither as an image of God nor as a center of conscious, willful thought and choice. The postmodern picture of the self is more like a jumbled, flickering movie collage, a screen on which society projects all kinds of changing, ultimately meaningless images. Some have called postmodernism's concept "the disappearing self." You can see why: if others determine everything you are, what's really left of *you*?

Thinking about the Self as a Christian

How ought a Christian respond to this postmodern idea of a disappearing self? The basic notion has a certain plausibility; it's only too obvious that much of what we think and feel is influenced, even determined, by our cultural surroundings. Accepting that can feel disorienting—but does it have to be a bad thing? On the other hand, it's certainly *not* obvious that social construction is the whole story about ourselves. In everyday life, there at least appears to be some room for free will and some more room for traits and tendencies that no amount of social conditioning could change. What exactly to embrace or reject about the postmodern (or modern, or premodern) vision of the self, and what lessons to draw is, on the whole, a puzzling question. What follows are some of my own thoughts.

First of all, a Christian need not be dismayed at the idea that she is shaped in very fundamental ways by her relations with others. That is, the bare fact that one's self is, to one degree or another, *constructed* shouldn't trouble us too much. It is a fundamental Christian idea that a relationship with one very important other person—God himself—exerts a singularly powerful transformative influence on a person, an influence that the Christian has every reason to embrace. That is a blow to modern dreams of autonomy, but it's a keystone of a Christian worldview.

However, the real worry that a postmodern vision of the self raises is not that you might be influenced by God, but that your very self is at the mercy of the culture at large, which mostly consists of impersonal or, worse, exploitative social forces: corporations, political parties, people with their own agenda. This fact of life—and, however postmoderns might exaggerate it, it is a fact of life—highlights the importance of monitoring the influences you allow closest to you. Christianity has a prescription for this problem: the church.

Believers in Jesus Christ are not supposed to operate freelance, hoisting themselves to spiritual heights using only their spiritual bootstraps. The church—the local congregation most immediately but also the wider body of believers, including especially people in positions of spiritual leadership—is the community intended to shape and form the character, the self, of a developing Christian. The common name for this task is *discipleship,* and it has at least four interpenetrating dimensions.

The church community is supposed to shape the *morals* of its members, inculcating Christian behavior in them. It should *teach,* shaping the minds of its members, giving them the tools of basic theology and a familiarity with the Bible. The church should give its members *spiritual formation* as well, nourishing the connection of each believer to God with spiritual practices, beginning with worship, prayer, and devotional Bible reading. Most fundamentally, perhaps, for reasons that will become clearer in the next chapter, the church gives its members *language.* Learning the stories and conceptual categories developed in the Christian tradition gives believers a peculiarly Christian way of thinking, a set of moral examples, and a frame in which to situate their own lives—in short, a worldview.

By objective measures, churches—in America, at any rate—are not doing a particularly good job on any of these fronts. Many people who claim Christianity are unfamiliar with Bible stories, like the stories of David and Saul, or basic theology, like the Incarnation. Few know the Ten Commandments. Attendance and giving are lower than they ought to be, prayer and Bible study are less frequent than they ought to be, and the moral differences between Christians and non-Christians are unremarkable.

Some of these failures, no doubt, are due to the weakness of churches. On the other hand, some might be due to a modern mind-set among contemporary Christians: a desire for autonomy, to run their own lives, and thus a tendency to treat the church as a place to gather for worship but not a place to have one's self transformed. I wonder if the root problem on both ends can be traced to a forgetfulness about the role of the church: that the church is part of God's plan for every Christian, that Christian selves are a work in progress that cannot be left to the culture at large, that discipleship is not an option for the spiritual elite but God's command for everyone.

The church, then, is the divine answer to the question of social construction of the self. Is there more to be said? Might a postmodern find something meaningful in the contingency of her self? Here I am only speculating, but there is a certain analogy between the idea that human beings are socially constructed, and the doctrine of the Trinity, so that one might connect being socially constructed with being made in the image of God. What do I mean? In classical Trinitarian theology, the divine persons (Father, Son, and Holy Spirit) are defined in terms of their relations with one another: the Father is the person who begets the Son and from whom the Spirit proceeds; the Son is the person who is begotten from the Father; the Spirit is the person who proceeds from the Father.[1] You can't define one of these divine persons without bringing them all into the definition. So it may be with us—each of us depends for our selfhood on others. In what is either a beautiful synthesis or a strange irony, perhaps postmodern thought can lead to a deeper appreciation of the Trinity!

At the end of the day, though, after a Christian has made as much peace as possible with the postmodern idea that our selves are deeply influenced by the society around us, she is still left with a traditional—and, I think, necessary—Christian emphasis on a real human nature. There is, says Christianity, an image of God in each human being and, arguably, also an ineradicable tendency to wrongdoing ("original sin" in theological language). Can this conviction be sustained in a postmodern world? Much postmodern opposition to the idea of a human nature is ethical—claiming that there is such a thing has harmful results. This argument leaves us in a position like the one we were in regarding moral absolutes—whether insisting on the existence of a human nature or denying it is more harmful is a serious question. Essence, like absolute truth, can be safety and freedom if it safeguards human dignity; denial of it can be slavery if it gives us no grounds to resist the tyranny of society.

Traditionally, it has been totalitarian states—particularly those based on Marx's ideas—that have explicitly subscribed to the idea that human beings are, in one form or another, entirely socially constructed. Since society determines what human beings are like, the thinking goes, any amount of social engineering is acceptable in the name of the collective good—there is no hard core of dignity to an individual human being that society has to respect. As history demonstrates, this attitude of a state toward its citizens is a recipe for misery. In North America, this kind of thinking reached its climax with the psychologist B. F. Skinner's behaviorism. Skinner taught that all human behavior was conditioned by experience, and he fantasized in novels and other writings about communal societies that effectively brainwashed their members into a perfect, peaceful social order. (One of Skinner's books is *Beyond Freedom and Dignity,* which wins my award for Most Chilling Book Title. I'll stick with freedom and dignity, thank you very much!)

Insisting that human beings share a human nature, that they all bear the image of God, is no guarantee of oppression. That assertion can be constructive or destructive, depending on how it is used. Using it to guard the rights and dignity of even the most vulnerable members of a society is a proper and constructive use. Using it to permit humans to exploit and degrade the environment, God's creation, on the grounds that no other creature is made in the image of God, is a destructive abuse. Knowing how to skillfully navigate this intersection between postmodernism and Christianity calls for wisdom.

Forming the Self

By now, it goes without saying that the self—the thoughts, feelings, and aspirations of a person—is influenced by many factors. Acknowledging this immediately leads to a problem: which influences should be pursued and embraced, and which should be rejected and avoided? As you might imagine, worldview has a lot to do with how one answers this question.

The modern person tries to live his life autonomously, controlling it through the exercise of his reason. It should go without saying that the only safe guides in this process are rational forms of thinking. Rational thinking proceeds according to rules and principles, where the paradigm is step-by-step logic. Thus, modernism respects whatever influences on the mind are logical, rational, and rule-bound; it denigrates whatever influences are not. Emotion, being illogical and unruly, is a distraction and a potential trap, so the modern person tries not to let emotion influence his decisions. Dramas, stories, and poetry have no rules and obey no logic, and therefore moderns don't think you can learn very much from them. On the other hand, careful reasoning in thought, word, or print is always worthy of attention.

Postmodern people, on the other hand, have lost faith in the power of reason. So they have no particular stake in step-by-step logic, rule-bound procedures, or in general what the modern would call rational thinking. This is not to say that they oppose it entirely, but it is one sort of influence among others. Postmoderns, like premoderns, can afford to be more open to different kinds of influences on the self. Emotion and the vehicles that produce it, like pictures, films, stories, plays, and poems, are not necessarily any less reliable, and are possibly more powerful, than logic and its vehicles, such as editorials, philosophical theories, sermons, or treatises of systematic theology. So, for instance, a sermon from Romans on the difference between the man under law and the man under grace may not make much impact, but a story illustrating the difference, like *Les Miserables,* might make an impression.

I noted in a previous chapter that evangelical services are oriented around the sermon, while a premodern service is oriented around the Eucharist. Here I'll note a second difference between these two types of service: I think that they are arranged with two different models in mind of how the self is most effectively formed. The modern, sermon-oriented service aims to shape its congregation through *teaching,* specifically, through hearing sermons that, over the course of years, cover the entire range of the Christian life. A premodern service has quite a different model. The liturgy has a number of prayers, summonses, and invocations that are repeated week after week; the year is divided into liturgical seasons that repeat year after year. The danger with this type of service is that it becomes stale with repetition. It is intended, however, as *practice.* Learning to live as a child of God, on this model, is less like learning history (from a book) and more like learning to ride a bike (from doing it over and over, including failures).

The difference between teaching and practice is simply one element of a wider difference about how the self is best formed in worship. Fundamentally, the question is, do people become better Christians through basically intellectual means, or do they need a heavy dose of nonintellectual influence? The latter option is the premodern answer—and, coming full circle, the postmodern answer too. All the elements of the premodern worship experience are designed to influence the believer in a God-ward direction. That explains why premodern cathedrals are architecturally impressive, why the music aims for grandeur, why the liturgy is conducted in elevated language, why the altar and liturgical implements are decorated for beauty and treated with reverence, and why parishioners in these churches sometimes genuflect or cross themselves. In contrast, modern-oriented low-church Protestants never bow or cross themselves, they simply close their eyes rather than kneel to pray in church, their architecture is unremarkable, their churches contain no visual art, and their music is relatively bland. The this-worldly elements of a modern Protestant service are designed to stay out of the way, to keep from interfering with the heart-to-heart, or mind-to-mind, communication between preacher and congregation, and between God and his people.

In a postmodern world, there is no particular reason that church services should remain the way they were instituted during the modern period. Some changes have already begun. As postmodern Christians have begun to arrange their own services, they typically juxtapose old and new elements, for example, using PowerPoint presentations in candlelight ceremonies. This kind of juxtaposition expresses a laudable desire to assimilate the best of the old and the new, reaching into both the past and the future without fear of either. One of the deep questions at stake in the design of a service, however, as I have been pointing out, is how you think about the self. Are people basically influenced through their reason, so that teaching should be the focus? Through their emotions, so that music and art should be emphasized? Through certain habitual patterns of activity, so that liturgical practices ought to be established? And how socially constructed are we, so that old and young, white and black and Latino, working class and middle class, modern and postmodern would benefit differently from different types of service? The contours of the postmodern self—if there is one single type that qualifies as "the postmodern self," and there probably isn't—are just beginning to be outlined. The worship of the future may look like nothing we have ever seen before. Or it may borrow a lot from the worship of premodern Christians.

For Further Thought

1. Make a list of every community or social circle you maintain contact with—include friends, family, relatives, colleagues, churches, volunteer organizations, Internet lists, and so on. Now make a similar list of communities that, say, a peasant at the time of the Reformation might have been involved in. What do the differences in these lists tell you?

2. Make a list of the means you can use to communicate with your friends (telephone, email, etc.). Now make a list of the means that, say, a peasant at the time of the Reformation could have used. What do the differences in these lists tell you?

3. Enumerate some ways that you think you are influenced by your social environment. This may be easier if you first think about how someone else is influenced and then ask the same questions about yourself.
4. Does the answer to the previous question bother you? Why or why not?
5. What are the attractions of autonomy? That is, why would anyone want it? See if you can articulate this clearly.
6. How does your church seek to influence the selves of its members? What could it do better?
7. What is the meaning of life?

Language and Thought

Language is perhaps the most remarkable human invention. To get a sense for just how remarkable language is, consider the competing claims of telepathy. Some people have thought they could telepathically communicate their thoughts to another person. Whenever telepathy is tested, however, it turns out that, at best, the communicated thoughts are vague and the technique is unreliable. You and I, however, have the ability to communicate our thoughts to other people in an extremely precise and reliable fashion, and we have had this ability since we were small children. It's easy: just say what's on your mind.

Once you realize how uniquely powerful language is, the question becomes, how does it work? How does language manage to capture our thoughts so precisely, and how does it manage to communicate truths (and falsehoods) about the world so accurately? The twentieth century—the late evening of the modern era and the early dawn of post-modernity—saw a profound transformation in the way philosophers answered this question. Without this transformation, postmodernism as it exists now could not have been born. In this chapter, we'll explore this shift in the understanding of language and its effects on related ideas: the mind, thinking, metaphor, knowledge, and learning. We'll also see how postmoderns employ these ideas in their own distinctive fashion.

Names or Games?

Until the twentieth century, people thought of language as made up of names. Names, like the word "Fido," refer to things, like the dog Fido. If you think about the way children learn language, the general idea is quite plausible for all kinds of words, not just obvious names like Fido. You point to Fido and say "Fido," and you point to a few tables and say "table," and you point to a series of red objects and say "red"; after a few tries, the child has learned how to use each word. The cases seem very similar. Each word, then, refers to a thing. "Fido," for instance, refers to a particular dog. "Table" refers to what all tables have in common, namely the quality of tablehood, while "red" refers to the quality of redness. A word like "justice" refers to an abstract entity that actual institutions and acts may or may not resemble. This approach is called the "Fido"-Fido theory of meaning because of its one-to-one relationship between words and things, and because, in the theory, all words are treated like names.

In the twentieth century, however, as philosophers and linguists began studying language more closely, the "Fido"-Fido theory of meaning began to look less and less plausible. The theory works pretty well for actual names, like "Fido"; it works less well for words like "table" or "red." And you may have found yourself wanting to get off the boat when I said that "justice" names an abstract entity. Words like "and," "ouch," and "perhaps" are even poorer candidates for being names: they don't seem to refer to anything at all. As these sorts of worries gained traction, the "Fido"-Fido theory lost adherents. In its place, a new picture of how language works came into favor.

The new approach to language compared language to a game, for instance, a game of chess. What defines a game as *chess* is not the shape or size of the pieces, but the rules the pieces follow. It would be a mistake to define a rook as "a piece of wood about two inches high, carved to look like a tower." Instead, a rook is a piece that follows certain rules: it begins the game in one of the corners of the board, and it is allowed to move vertically or horizontally until another piece blocks it. Words, on this theory, are similar: what makes words mean what they do are the rules surrounding their use. For instance, there is a rule that you say "perhaps" when you aren't sure, and another rule that you say "ouch" when you are in pain. The rules governing "and" are rules of inference: from "Paul had glaucoma" together with "Paul had bowlegs" you can infer that "Paul had glaucoma *and* bowlegs," and vice versa. Similarly, there are linguistic rules about what things count as red, or as tables, and there are rules of inference like "if something is red then it is colored" and "if something is a table it has legs."

These two different theories of language have dramatically different consequences in a whole range of areas. In the next few sections, we'll explore these differences. We'll also see how the idea of language games has influenced postmodernism.

The Mind and Its Concepts

Because language is used to express thoughts, approaches to language have important consequences for how one thinks about the mind. One important consequence lies in what it means to think a true thought. If you are thinking, "Sylvester is a cat," then "Sylvester" names a particular animal, "cat" names the quality of cathood, and your thought is true if that animal does in fact have that quality. The cathood is "out there" in the world just as surely as the cat is, and both Sylvester and his quality of cathood are named in the sentence and reflected in the thought. The words in the sentence mirror the objects in the world, and the thought that the sentence expresses mirrors the world too. Perfect knowledge is simply this mirroring process taken to the umpteenth degree. The job of the mind is to mirror nature, presenting a faultless reflection of the way the world is.

Another important consequence involves how we understand concepts, the categories like "cat," "red," and "justice," that our minds use. On the "Fido"-Fido theory, concepts don't change with time. The word "cat" has named cats since it was invented (unless, of course, we were to deliberately stipulate that it was to name something else, say, goldfish); likewise, for "red" and "justice." Thus, the use of these words has expressed the same thoughts from time immemorial. We may call different things "just" now than we used to, but that does not indicate a shifting concept of "justice" or a change in the meaning of the word "justice." It is simply a reevaluation of what things *are* just.

Several important corollaries follow from the static, unchanging character of concepts. First, the concepts we use are necessary. We could do without them only at the price of being unable to think certain (true) thoughts. Second, they are natural: they correspond to objects in the world. Finally, mere thinking—simply *using* concepts—has no ethical ramifications, or no bad ones at any rate. Thinking could not, fundamentally, be done with any other categories than the ones we have.

Thinking of language as a game, analogous to chess, creates a vastly different picture of the mind and its concepts. The categories of thing-in-the-world, concept-in-the-mind, and word-in-the-language are no longer tied together in a tight bundle of one-to-one correspondence. Consequently, we can't think of the mind as reflecting the world, as if in a mirror. Instead, we have to begin by understanding the many ways that concepts are related to one another. "Cat," for instance, is not a name for a semi-mysterious quality, cathood, but rather a word bound up in a "language game" with other words like "animal," "mammal," "tabby," and so forth. Corresponding to this network of words is a network of concepts, called a *conceptual scheme*. The concepts "mammal" and "animal" are, so to speak, above the concept "cat" (since if Sylvester is a cat, he's also a mammal and an animal); the concepts "tabby" and "Abyssinian" are below it (since if Sylvester is a tabby, or an Abyssinian, he's a cat). The concepts "dog," "chipmunk," "lizard," and so on are opposed to it (since if Sylvester is one of these, he's not a cat, and vice versa). To contemplate something as simple as "Sylvester is a cat," therefore, involves the thinker in this whole apparatus. The mind can no more think "Sylvester is a cat" in isolation than you could move a solitary tower-shaped piece across a board marked with squares, and call it a move in a chess game.

Clearly, this particular conceptual scheme—the one including the concept "cat" and the network of concepts surrounding it—depends heavily on the science of biology. Consequently, the concepts incorporated in this scheme are not necessary: if our science had developed differently, the conceptual scheme would reflect that difference. Nor is the conceptual scheme natural: it doesn't simply reflect the world around us, but it includes a heavy theoretical component. For example, while "cat" is a more or less obvious category, "mammal," which groups cats with whales and bats and humans, is something only a zoologist would come up with. Yet these two concepts are closely related—it's common knowledge that cats are mammals.

Furthermore, since a conceptual scheme is neither natural nor necessary, it is socially constructed, and could have been constructed differently. This makes using a conceptual scheme a matter of moral concern, at least potentially. Probably "cat" is not a concept that will raise any eyebrows, but other biological or quasi-biological concepts, like "intelligence quotient," lend themselves to ethical scrutiny. Questions like these raise their heads: Why do we think there is a biological component to intelligence? What does it mean to say someone is "intelligent" anyway? Is that something you can measure on a standardized test? Insofar as these questions have any bite, they call into question not merely beliefs but entire ways of thinking and making divisions between people—entire conceptual schemes. In fact, our way of understanding natural intelligence has changed over the course of the twentieth century, and the name of a well-known standardized test reflects this change. From 1941 until recently, SAT was an acronym for "Scholastic Aptitude Test." The test was supposed to measure native intelligence—in particular, a student's natural aptitude for college. Since it actually measures no such thing, in 1990 the name was changed to "Scholastic Assessment Test." But since 1994, the name of the test has simply been "SAT," three letters that don't stand for anything. The increasing meaninglessness of the acronym reflects a growing dissatisfaction with the concept of natural, biologically given intelligence.

The change from thinking of language as names to thinking of language as games, and only one or a few of many possible games—and the associated change from thinking of our concepts as necessary and natural to thinking of them as invented and changeable—draws out a familiar critique from postmoderns. Conceptual schemes (a different name for these would be "worldviews"—large-scale ways of looking at the world) are a form, quite literally, of thought control. They constrain the sorts of thoughts you can form and the lines of investigation you can pursue. Not that we could hope to *eliminate* such constraints—that would be like trying to invent a board game in which there were no rules for the movement of the pieces. But postmoderns are suspicious of "ordinary" (that is, received or traditional) ways of thinking and talking because any received way of thinking or talking is a form of power exercised by the past over the present. It is a version of reliance on tradition.

The postmodern response is to resist the language games and conceptual schemes taken for granted in the wider culture. Postmodern authors will consciously attempt to use language in atypical, even bizarre ways, in order to challenge their readers' way of thinking. If you have ever had occasion to read postmodern writing, especially writing of an academic bent, you may have thought it hard to follow. It *is* hard to follow; and sometimes the difficulty is deliberate. An example, for your enjoyment, is a passage from the French postmodern philosopher Jacques Derrida:

> In *Glas*, the pieces [you know that it is an organ score in pieces (bits or bites detached either by the teeth, coated in saliva, and then half swallowed and then thrown up, or by the fingernails and then left in hairy shreds)] that could be called "theoretical," the "theses," the "dissertations" (on dialectics and galactics, on absolute knowledge, the *Sa*

and the Immaculate Conception, the *IC*, on the stricture of the general economy, on the appeal of the proper name or nomenclature in the class struggle, on the limits of the Freudian or Marxist theory of fetishism, phallogocentrism, on the logic of the signifier, on the logic of antherection or obsequence, on the anthoedipus and castration, on the arbitrariness of the sign and the so-called proper name, on mimesis and the so-called impulsional bases of phonation, on the faceless figure of the mother, on language, sublimation, the family, the State, religion, mourning-work, feminine sexuality, the colossos, the double bind—the double band—and schizophrenia, and so forth) all of these "theoretical" morsels are processions tattooed, incised, inlaid into the bodies of the two colossi or the two bands which are stuck on and woven into each other, at the same time clinging to each other and sliding one over the other in a dual unity without any relation to self.[1]

Whew!

Literal and Figurative Language

Another important upshot of the "Fido"-Fido theory of meaning is a sharp distinction between metaphorical and literal uses of language. Names work pretty straightforwardly. "Fido" refers to Fido, and if there is more than one Fido around, context tells us which one is meant. Since according to the "Fido"-Fido theory each word in a sentence is a name, there is always a precise fact of the matter about what a sentence literally means. Figurative senses are created when names are taken to refer to something other than what they really refer to. Used literally, "Sylvester is a cool cat" means that Sylvester is a feline at low temperature; metaphorically, however, it may mean that Sylvester is a stylish person. Furthermore, there is always some literal expression of what a metaphor means. That is, if you use a metaphor, you could have said the same thing nonmetaphorically simply by using the ordinary name ("stylish person") for whatever you used the metaphorical name ("cool cat") for.

Thinking of words as positions in a game rather than as names of objects breaks down this sharp division between literal and figurative senses. If you say, "Sylvester is a cool cat," are you simply speaking figuratively, or are you recommending a change in the conceptual scheme surrounding "cat"? If the answer to that question seems too obvious, consider, "She dropped her needle," "She dropped her hem," "She dropped her eyes," "She dropped the subject." Where does the literal sense end and the metaphor begin? A believer in language games thinks there is no sharp line to be drawn.

For a postmodern concerned about the potentially oppressive power embodied in a received conceptual scheme, this fluidity between literal and metaphorical language is an opportunity to be exploited. Using language in metaphorical ways creates new connections of thought that would be difficult or impossible to represent according to the rules of the usual conceptual scheme. (Think about it: language is not *literally* a game, but how else would you describe this view of it?) Poetic language breaks the lock of literal meaning and allows thoughts to arise that previously were literally unthinkable. Metaphor is the postmodern tool of conceptual liberation. Derrida is attempting something like this in the quote above, comparing his "theses" to bites of food and tattoos. Successful or not, his aim is to give his reader new conceptions of theses. Over time, however, as new notions become familiar, the once-metaphorical usage can harden into literal usage, or "common sense." Thus we get "dead metaphors": dropped subjects, depressed economies, levels of discussion, attractive theories, language games, worldviews . . . and dead metaphors.

Facts and Interpretations

Finally, the "Fido"-Fido theory lends itself to a sharp distinction between facts and interpretations, or (what comes to much the same thing) between observations and theories. The idea is that some things that words name are immediately perceptible: cats, for instance, are like this. Other things are not immediately perceptible and can only be known by inference: chemical compounds, for example, are like this. The fact/interpretation distinction, then, has to do with our knowledge: facts are known directly and for certain, while interpretations require some inference from the facts and so are less certain. For instance, "The thermometer reads 100 degrees" is a factual statement, or observation—we can see this just by looking. "Water is made up of hydrogen and oxygen" is an interpretation, or theory, based on data like chemistry experiments. Interpretations are supposed to be less well known than facts: you will hear, "That's just your interpretation" or "That's only a theory," but never, "That's only a fact."

Language games and conceptual schemes, however, upset this simple picture of knowledge and erode the sharp line between facts and interpretations. One important consequence is that no statement can ever be absolutely, finally known to be true. An illustration from grade-school science will help. Suppose you want to find out at what temperature water boils—you know it's supposed to be 212°F, but you just want to prove this elementary scientific fact for yourself. This is an easy experiment to run, right? You put a pot of water on the stove, wait for it to boil, and stick in a thermometer. But let's imagine that, when you take the thermometer out, it reads 211°. Now what conclusion do you draw?

One option is to think that the scientists have been wrong all along and that water really does boil at 211°, not 212°. That is, you could adjust your "theory" about the boiling temperature of water to accord with the "fact" that your thermometer reports. Another option is to think that you must have misread the thermometer—you could question the "fact" because of your knowledge of the "theory." Or perhaps the thermometer is flawed. Or maybe it cooled one degree between the time you took it out of the water and the time you read it. Maybe the water is impure, or the altitude has affected the reading, or a local weather anomaly has disturbed the experiment. And so on—there is no end to the list of conclusions you *could* draw from this relatively simple experiment. That is because the concepts "water," "thermometer," "temperature," "boil," "air pressure," "altitude," and others are bound up in a complicated tangle of relationships: you can conclude nearly anything if you are willing to make enough adjustments elsewhere. Some adjustments are more reasonable than others, perhaps. But the point remains that whether or not water boils at 212° is never *finally* established—there is always *some* story we could tell that would explain all the data and yet have water boiling at some other temperature. Therefore, no sharp line can be drawn between what we know for certain ("facts"), and what we infer from other things we know ("interpretations"). Facts and interpretations bleed into one another.

Postmoderns take the vague boundary between "fact" and "interpretation" and draw some startling conclusions. With no sharp distinction between fact and interpretation, or between evidence and conjecture, they see no reason to fully trust anyone's assertions about anything. No assertion really counts as unassailable knowledge; all statements are merely provisional, contestable claims—one person's account competing with everyone else's. Furthermore, the very terms in which a statement is phrased—the language game, or conceptual scheme, in which it figures—are only one option among many. Since these games and schemes are invented, we might well invent different ones.

This is the theoretical underpinning for postmodern relativism, discussed in chapters three and four. There is nothing stable in the postmodern intellectual picture: no concepts we can't reform, no facts we can't reinterpret. How we choose to view our world, then, is to some extent a matter of preference, and the intense social forces shaping our minds mold our preferences. The most subtle, most pervasive influence on our minds is language itself. For it is the language games we learn as children that impress upon our minds the conceptual schemes we use in our thinking. We have seen how postmoderns fundamentally distrust the social influences that shape our selves, particularly our thinking selves; and from the postmodern perspective, language is one more untrustworthy, but unusually powerful, influence. Consequently, postmoderns attempt to combat its influence with metaphorical language, new jargon, obfuscatory prose, and self-referential irony.

Two Short Examples

The idea that language shapes thought is a particularly important postmodern idea. I want to give two quick examples—more readily intelligible than Derrida's quote—that illustrate the point.

Exhibit A is (or was) the use in English of masculine forms like "man," "he," and "him" to stand for persons of either gender. Thus, it has been considered proper grammar to say, "Everyone should take responsibility for *his* own actions." This has the effect, a postmodern would claim, of making males the favored gender: women become like an exception to the rule. Now, a traditionalist would reply, "Nonsense! There's no favoritism—that's just a rule of grammar!" The assumption in this reply is that rules of grammar cannot exhibit favoritism or bias; they are the neutral rules governing a neutral medium for conveying thoughts. But this is an assumption that postmodernism would deny. Grammatical rules aren't handed down by God, and they don't spring out of the ground—they're neither necessary nor natural. They're human inventions, in fact, rules for a certain sort of social interaction (the kind that involves speaking and listening, or writing and reading). As such, they can exhibit all the partiality and prejudice of any rules for social interaction. If there can be unjust laws, there can be unjust grammars. Like truth, morality, and essence, for a postmodern, grammar is power: whoever controls the rules and ordinary usages of a language controls what can be thought. Changing the way people talk allows people to *think* things that previously were literally unthinkable. For example, if I start writing, "Everyone should take responsibility for *her* own actions," this may introduce a subtle jarring effect, a stimulus to new ways of conceiving the relationship between women and men.

Exhibit B is (or was) a stylistic rule. It used to be taught, and in some circles still is taught, that an author should never refer to herself in formal written work; in a crunch, she could write, "this author." Nor was the author supposed to refer to the reader as "you"; instead, "the reader" was marginally acceptable. You, the reader, will note that

I, the author, have been flouting these rules from page one. There is no obvious reason for them—every work has an author, and works are always read by (who else?) readers. So why shouldn't an author write "I" and "you"?

The reasoning behind the rule has to do with certain modern sensibilities. Knowledge, for a modern, is impersonal: the facts are just "out there," the same for everyone, equally accessible to anyone with rational faculties. Objectivity is achieved through abstracting from any peculiarities of my situation or yours. Insofar as a work refers to the author or the reader, it comes across to a modern as "subjective"—*merely* personal, not *fully* rational. To a modern, a proper piece of writing should be as impersonal and impartial as Truth and Reason itself.

Postmoderns, in contrast, consider this sensibility deceptive. It's not as if there isn't an author to a text, just because she isn't mentioned. The text remains a particular person's point of view, with all the partiality and limitations of perspective that entails, even if it's not presented that way. It's not as if the reader isn't there either, just because the author doesn't talk to him directly. Books don't exist in a vacuum, they exist to be read. Those readers don't vanish just because they aren't mentioned.

In this book, then, you are getting my take on postmodernism. I'm writing as clearly and accurately as I can, but after all, it's only my perspective. This book would remain a book from my perspective even if I wrote it in a different, more formal style. The question you have to answer is, how much of what I'm saying about postmodernism do you believe? How much of my perspective on postmodernism will you adopt? You would have to answer this question even if I adopted a more authoritative tone than I have, and even if I left out this paragraph. You and I are just being open and honest about it.

For Further Thought

1. Pick a page from a book at random, or listen closely to your friends, and count the metaphors.

2. Can you come up with an example of how language is used in ways that restrict or distort understanding of an issue?

3. Do you think there is a difference between "facts" and "interpretations"? If so, give examples of each, and try to explain the difference (without using the words "fact" or "interpretation"). If not, explain why so many people think there is a difference.

4. Do you think there is a difference between "facts" and "values"? If so, give examples of each, and try to explain the difference (without using the words "fact" or "value"). If not, explain why so many people think there is a difference.

Inquiry and Interpretation

For postmoderns, no knowledge is fully reliable and no concepts are absolutely indispensable. This makes the postmodern understanding of the search for knowledge, or *inquiry*—that is, what goes on in the various intellectual disciplines such as history, physics, chemistry, psychology, and theology—quite different from the modern understanding of it. The premodern understanding, as we shall see, was different yet.

One form of inquiry is the interpretation of texts. "Text," in postmodern parlance, means nearly anything that can be interpreted, including books, speeches, Bible passages, magazine covers, or the ritual at the Tomb of the Unknown Soldier; and this is how I will use the word. The postmodern approach to inquiry of all kinds affects, among many other things, how postmoderns interpret texts and how they evaluate others' interpretation of texts. This chapter begins, then, by outlining how the idea of inquiry has changed through the premodern, modern, and postmodern periods. Then it goes on to address what this change means for textual interpretation, in particular, the interpretation of the Bible.

Premodern Inquiry: the Constraints of Authority and the Love of God

Inquiry—by which I mean learning, investigation, education, and the pursuit of knowledge in general—has a history. That is, how people have understood and approached inquiry has changed over time. The different conceptions of inquiry vary on two accounts. First, they include different motives for inquiring; they construe the *point* of knowledge differently. Second, they have different understandings of what *validates* our knowledge, in other words, what standards must be met in order for a particular belief to count as knowledge.

For premoderns (more precisely, for medieval western Europeans) knowledge was oriented, ultimately, toward the love of God and the love of neighbor. A university education included grammar, rhetoric, and dialectic, three subjects that trained the mind to understand arguments and follow lines of reasoning. It also included, at a second level, geometry, arithmetic, astronomy, and music, which further trained the mind and enabled the learner to appreciate the orderliness of God's creation. All of these disciplines were a preparation for theology, "queen of the sciences," the study of God himself. The point of theology, in turn, was both to learn about God and to draw the learner closer to God. These two goals were closely related: mature faith, including spiritual sensitivity and a finely tuned moral character, was considered necessary in order to understand the deeper things of God. So you could not accurately know about God without also knowing God in a more personal sense. And of course you could not teach others about God, thus benefiting them, without knowing God yourself.

In short, in the premodern worldview, knowledge is only one part of a whole package whose ultimate aim is a rela-

tionship with God and others. Intellectual understanding
and the inquiry that leads to it is good, but only as part
of the package. The proper motive behind inquiry was
love. The medieval monk Bernard of Clairvaux summed
up this understanding in a sermon, "The Acquiring of
Knowledge":

> For there are some who long to know for the sole purpose
> of knowing, and that is shameful curiosity; others who long
> to know in order to become known, and that is shameful
> vanity. . . . There are others still who long for knowledge
> in order to sell its fruits for money or honors, and this is
> shameful profiteering; others again who long to know in
> order to be of service, and this is charity. Finally there are
> those who long to know in order to benefit themselves,
> and this is wisdom. Of all these categories, only the last
> two avoid the abuse of knowledge, because they desire to
> know for the purpose of doing good.

Because the premodern's motive for pursuing knowledge
was the pursuit of God, church authority constrained the
directions that inquiry could take. In the premodern worldview, nothing could count as knowledge that was inconsistent with the Bible and the authoritative theology worked
out from the Bible. Thus, every now and then a bishop
would feel the necessity of condemning a set of philosophical or theological theses, and such a condemnation simply
foreclosed that direction of inquiry for faithful Christians.
The bishop of Paris issued such a condemnation in 1277,
intending to curtail the speculations of over-eager Aristo-
telians, and in 1521 the pope attempted to restrain Martin
Luther in the same way. By that time, however, as we have
seen, Luther and others who would shortly participate in
what would become known as the Protestant Reformation

were no longer willing to accept the restrictions on inquiry that church authority laid down.

Modern Inquiry: "Science for Science's Sake"

When the modern period began, the acknowledged motive behind inquiry was not dramatically different from the premodern motive. Francis Bacon had written in his 1605 book, *The Advancement of Learning,* that knowledge was to be pursued "for the glory of the Creator and the relief of man's estate." As modernity wore on and Christian faith waned, "the glory of the Creator" dropped out of the equation, but the general idea that knowledge aimed at the material and moral progress of humanity persisted. It was only much later in modernity, when disillusionment about the connection between scientific progress and moral advance had set in, that even this motive was dismissed as naïve. Instead, knowledge was to be pursued for its own sake. Summing up this idea, Max Weber wrote,

> What is the attitude of the academic man towards his vocation—that is, if he is at all in quest of such a personal attitude? He maintains that he engages in "science for science's sake" and not merely because others, by exploiting science, bring about commercial or technical success.

That quote is from Weber's 1918 lecture, "Science as a Vocation." What Bernard of Clairvaux would have criticized as "shameful curiosity"—"long[ing] to know for the sole purpose of knowing"—had become, for Weber, the stated aim of academic research. Weber's influence shaped the university systems of Europe and North America so that "pure research," unmoored from any practical application or especially from any spiritual refinement, remains a high academic value today.

Moderns, as we have seen, consistently rejected the constraints of traditional authority, and this affected the modern conception of inquiry. Intellectuals of the Enlightenment and afterward regarded traditional theology, the sort that appealed to the authoritative revelation of the Bible or the dogmas of the church, as only dubiously a branch of knowledge, belonging in a university. It was certainly not "the queen of the sciences." Genuine knowledge, moderns thought, was the sort that depended not on any authority, but only on the individual—the observations of his senses and the reasoning of his intellect.

This ideal was ultimately cast into the "scientific method," the modern gold standard for knowledge. In its most basic terms, an investigator operating by this method begins by assembling data (the facts), and then impartially and objectively derives a conjecture (the interpretation) from the data. In the best cases—for instance, chemistry experiments—other investigators can check the data and arrive at the same conclusion. How closely a discipline approaches this ideal of knowledge can be measured by how checkable its data are and how much consensus investigators in the field achieve. This yardstick makes physics and chemistry (the "hard sciences") the highest, most secure forms of knowledge; further down the scale (in approximate order) come biology, economics, psychology, sociology, history, philosophy, theology, and literary and art criticism.

Postmodern Inquiry: Narratives of Power

In the last chapter, I used a trivial science experiment to explain how, once you accept the picture of language as a game, no investigation can ever establish a truth beyond *all* doubt. I said there that *some* story could explain all the data and yet draw a different conclusion from the usual one, namely that water boils at 212°. This story would emphasize how careful you were in conducting the experiment and controlling for outside factors to justify the conclusion that water boils at 211°. The more conventional story, in contrast, would cite the reliability of scientific authorities to justify its conclusion (whatever the actual thermometer reading) that water boils at 212°. The fact that these justifications are stories—narratives of events—is significant for postmoderns. It means that no scientific endeavor—or more generally, no inquiry—depends on evidence alone. Conclusions always rest on more than evidence, because evidence doesn't speak for itself. It has to be interpreted, and this interpretation always includes an element of storytelling. What goes for elementary chemistry experiments goes for any other kind of rational investigation: historians drawing conclusions about the past, sociologists drawing conclusions about contemporary society, theologians making inferences about God, or farmers deciding on the best methods of agriculture.

Postmoderns push this insight as far as possible. (Some would say they push it even further.) Since any question in chemistry, history, theology, agriculture, or any other discipline admits multiple answers, depending on which interpretation of the evidence you find convincing, postmoderns have lost faith in the idea of objective verification. Instead, they focus on the persuasive power of the stories we tell about, for instance, how reliable our scientists are, how careful our investigations were, how impartial we tried to be, and the like. Thus, for a postmodern all disciplines produce a form of literature, and what a modern would call analyzing the evidence, postmoderns consider a version of literary criticism. The results of any inquiry carry as much weight as the results of any other literary criticism, so there is no solid, factual knowledge in the sense a modern would expect. Instead, there are simply competing interpretive narratives. A disciplinary consensus, like the widespread agreement that water boils at 212°, is for a postmodern simply a dominant interpretation, a kind of intellectual monopoly.

Literature, not science or theology, is the master discipline, the paradigm of inquiry, for postmoderns. And in the last analysis, persuasive narrative, not scientific method, validates a belief as knowledge for postmoderns. Finally, for a postmodern the motive behind inquiry is neither the pursuit of God nor the pursuit of knowledge for its own sake. Rather, the pursuit of knowledge is, in postmodern eyes, the pursuit of power. The ability to stand as an intellectual authority, with the clout to determine what counts as knowledge and what does not, is a form of power, as we saw in chapter four. A postmodern, sensitive to the dangers inherent in concentrated power, tends to resist intellectual consensus. Therefore, she tries to open up different interpretations of the evidence, intellectual narratives that will compete with the usual ones. Confronted with our water-boiling experiment, she might embrace an interpretation of it that argues that water boils at 211°, if for no other reason than that such an interpretation challenges the accepted view.

Interpreting the Bible

One kind of inquiry, especially important for Christians, is determining what the words of the Bible mean. Biblical interpretation is a particularly clear and instructive lens through which to view the differences in the premodern, modern, and postmodern approaches to inquiry and knowledge. Questions of biblical interpretation press all sorts of interesting and important buttons: premoderns' conception of theology as the highest kind of knowledge, moderns' dependence on reason and rejection of authority, and postmoderns' concern with the power of entrenched interpretations.

I mentioned above that, according to the premodern worldview, a mature spirituality was necessary to understand the deeper aspects of faith; the deeper the understanding sought, the greater the need for maturity. This general thought comes from Paul, for example, when he writes, "The man without the Spirit does not accept the things that come from the Spirit of God, for they are foolishness to him, and he cannot understand them, because they are spiritually discerned."[1] In practice, this attitude meant that not just anyone was considered competent to interpret the scriptures. Interpretation was a task best left to those men recognized as having special spiritual stature, in particular, the church fathers and certain wise theologians since them. Thus, the typical Bible of the late Middle Ages was the *Glossa Ordinaria,* a book that placed the biblical text in the center of the page and surrounded it by commentary from eminent Christians of the past. The commentary didn't have the same authority as the Bible itself, but it did carry considerable prestige. Ordinary priests or monks, much less ordinary laypersons, weren't expected to contradict these traditional interpretations. The reason, of course, was: who are you to disagree with the fathers of the church?

By the time of the Enlightenment, it was clear that *somebody* was getting the Bible wrong. Catholics, Lutherans, Calvinists, and Anabaptists differed over scripture's meaning in important ways. The more radical versions of *sola Scriptura* encouraged individual believers to interpret the Bible for themselves, which meant that they disagreed about it. Confronted with conflicting interpretations, people had to choose sides in ways they never had before. In this confused milieu (which hasn't left us), it was inevitable that someone would try to approach the Bible in a completely neutral, objective, even scientific spirit, to determine what it really meant.

In 1670, Baruch Spinoza published his *Theological-Political Treatise,* one of the first books to advocate reading the Bible in a spirit entirely free of religious presuppositions. He wrote,

> I deliberately resolved to examine Scripture afresh, conscientiously and freely, and to admit nothing as its teaching which did not most clearly derive from it.[2]

Spinoza was an unorthodox Jew whose religious views inclined to pantheism. His biblical interpretations, unsurprisingly, are unorthodox too: the prophets teach us morality but nothing else; the Hebrew people were "chosen" only in the sense that God chose them to live in a certain territory; miracles cannot violate the laws of nature.

Spinoza is perhaps the first truly modern biblical interpreter. He assumes that he needs nothing but his own reason to correctly understand the Bible—his reading will be simply "fresh, conscientious and free." From Spinoza's modern perspective, the fact that his interpretations diverge so fundamentally from more traditional readings of the Bible is simply evidence that tradition is a source of prejudice and unclear thinking. From the premodern perspective, on the other hand, it is no wonder that Spinoza, without the assistance of the Holy Spirit or a lively Christian faith, got the meaning of the Bible so wrong. During the modern period, Spinoza's side of this debate prevailed. Many other biblical scholars would come after him, and few would agree with all his conclusions. Nearly all modern scholars, even up to the present day, however, have accepted Spinoza's interpretive assumption: that understanding the scriptures required no special spiritual equipment. Reason alone, or reason assisted by scientific research, especially in fields like history or archaeology, would provide an increasingly accurate understanding of the Bible.

Characteristically, postmoderns distrust the goal of accuracy—that is, the idea that one interpretation of a scripture passage should be presented as *the* meaning. Postmodern relativism on this point is on a level with postmodern relativism about meanings in general: the meanings of particular texts depend on the language game the reader is playing, that is, the conceptual scheme and background assumptions that the reader brings to the text. The modern emphasis on accuracy is, to postmodern eyes, simply a way of establishing an interpretive monopoly, a process that, as often as not, justifies the interpreter's preferred conclusions. Postmoderns believe that practically any interpretation can be justified by some construal of the evidence, so the question "Is this interpretation accurate?" is not the main point. Instead, other questions, like "Is this interpretation liberating?" or "Does this interpretation advance the cause of justice?" come to the fore.

Moreover, this multiplication of meanings is a good thing for another reason, in postmodern eyes. It prevents dominant narratives from restricting our interpretive options. So, for instance, you can read the story of Adam and Eve's expulsion from the garden of Eden as an account of the fall from perfection of the original members of the human race; or you can read it as a metaphor for every human's position before God; or you can read it, more darkly, as a critique of God's arbitrary ways toward humankind. Jesus's crucifixion can be interpreted as an atoning sacrifice for

sin, as a moral example for all people, as an instance of the
unjust suffering pervasive in the world, or as a particularly
horrible case of child abuse. Which position you take will
be determined by the conceptual scheme you bring to the
story and the kinds of narratives you find persuasive. Let
a thousand flowers bloom.

Thus, for a postmodern the meaning of a text lies ultimately in the hands of its reader. If this seems bizarre, it
may help to think back to the analogy between language
and chess. The rules of chess are not determined by anything in the nature of the pieces—the connection between
"looks like a tower" and "moves like a rook" is entirely
arbitrary—but by a broad social agreement among chess
players. However, anyone, at any time, can modify this
agreement. If you want, you can play chess with slightly
different rules; you can radically alter the rules and play
a game like checkers; or you can simply juggle the pieces,
playing no game at all. Likewise, the rules for interpreting texts—the linguistic usages, conceptual scheme, and
worldview employed when reading—are not sitting there
in the text itself but are brought to the text by its readers,
and they can be changed too, in mild or in radical ways.
There is nothing sacred about an interpretive framework,
for a postmodern, any more than there is anything sacred
about the particular rules common in the chess community.
Indeed, postmoderns believe that an entrenched interpretive
framework is likely to mask biases and restrict thought.
To think of one reader's interpretation as more accurate
than another's, therefore, is a modern superstition. You
can protest that some other person's interpretation is not
what you, or most people, would come up with . . . but,
well, so what? You can also say it is not what the author
intended. But again, so what? The author doesn't have
any more interpretive authority over the text—any more

of a monopoly on its meaning—than Spinoza, or you, or anyone else.

Christians, Postmodernism, and Biblical Interpretation

Undoubtedly the most troubling aspect of this chapter for Christians will be the consequences of postmodernism's view of interpreting the Bible. The Bible is an irreplaceable resource for "teaching, rebuking, correcting, and training in righteousness,"[3] and we need some notion of a stable meaning to scripture if any of those things is going to happen. Scriptural interpretation is a large and deep topic, and many people have written more and better on it than I ever will or could; nevertheless, I want to suggest a way out of the worries this chapter has raised.

Many Protestants have a recognizably modern approach to interpreting the Bible—or at least they say they do. They take for granted that the Bible speaks clearly, at least in essentials, and therefore that any layperson of normal intelligence can pick it up and understand it with fair accuracy. This attitude explains why, for instance, one Protestant method of evangelism is simply to hand out copies of the New Testament.

This attitude coexists with a sort of premodern practice. Serious Bible study, especially by pastors preparing sermons, usually involves consulting one or more commentaries, or in other words, appeals to a tradition of interpretation. The contemporary study Bible, chock-full of notes and cross-references, bears more than a passing resemblance to the *Glossa Ordinaria*. And it doesn't take too much self-awareness to realize that your theological environment, from church or childhood, heavily influences your take on difficult parts of scripture like the books of Romans or Revelation.

It is not as if contemporary Christians don't depend on traditions or authorities to understand the Bible. *Which* authorities they rely on have changed since premodern times; they depend a lot less on Augustine and Irenaeus, and a lot more on various seminary professors and pastors of large churches. Spinoza didn't shake his dependence on others either, however much he thought he did; his conclusions are noticeably influenced by the intellectual climate of his day and the thinkers he admired, not to mention his political preferences. In short, the modern approach to reading the Bible—Spinoza's interpretation made "afresh, conscientiously and freely, admit[ting] nothing as its teaching which did not most clearly derive from it"—is self-deceptive: there is no wholly impartial, assumption-free approach to the Bible or any other text. Always an inherited worldview, a set of background presuppositions, shapes the way a reader understands the material in front of him. Postmoderns and premoderns find common ground on this point.

Although I am criticizing the modern perspective on biblical interpretation, a perspective that many contemporary Christians share, I am *not* advocating reading the Bible in a careless, biased, and blinkered spirit. Rather, once we acknowledge how the condition of our minds and souls influences our reading of the Bible, we can become more self-conscious about the limits of our own interpretive abilities and about who we rely on to assist us in understanding the scriptures. Premodern Christianity was careful about this: only men (rarely women) of acknowledged spiritual stature were authorized to interpret the Bible. We, in a postmodern era, can at least consciously reflect on which voices we listen to and the criteria we use in choosing those voices. And this may mean that some of the *actual* criteria we currently use—such as "Dr. So-and-so's book is at the top of the best-seller list," or "Everyone else in my church reads Pastor Whoozit"—get treated more skeptically.

If the modern perspective on biblical interpretation can't stand, then we are confronted with two alternatives: a reach back into the past to premodern approaches, or forward into the future to postmodern ones. It's worth exploring the consequences of each. There are three interlocking points of contrast between the two options: their view of character, their view of authority, and their view of community, all as they relate to the process of understanding God's word.

A starting point of premodern thought about the Bible was that one had to be spiritually mature to understand it right. In other words, the Bible and the faith of the Christian community had to shape the reader before the reader could fully understand the Bible. Consequently, only those people deeply shaped by the Bible were allowed to interpret the Bible for others, and everyone else was expected to submit to these authorities. However, judging which people qualified for this task was in turn a matter of measuring their character and wisdom against the standards of the Bible, so that no one would be considered an authority who interpreted the Bible in a dramatically different way than what had gone before. The whole process was geared toward preserving a theological heritage, especially the biblical insights of past generations, and its result was a relatively tight community with widely shared assumptions about what the Bible had to say. Community was bought at the price of acknowledged authority.

The contrast with postmodern thought could not be sharper. Postmoderns agree with moderns that no special spiritual qualifications are required to interpret the Bible correctly. Their reasons diverge from modern reasons, however, in that postmoderns don't subscribe to the ideal of "correctness" at all. Consequently, there is no such thing as an authority on the Bible, in the postmodern scheme, and therefore no need to submit one's own understanding to such an authority. In fact, postmodern approaches to any text emphasize breaking free of traditional interpretations. As a result, no postmodern will follow in the footsteps of any other interpreter of scripture; to do so would be to miss the point. For postmoderns, the great goal is freedom, especially freedom of thought, which a postmodern equates with original thought. A desire for original thought, however, translates into a fear of being influenced. This obsession with originality and freedom, in turn, entails that postmoderns ultimately risk failing to communicate altogether. When deeply idiosyncratic interpretations run sharply against the obvious grain of the text, even deliberately obscuring their own attempted contribution, readers find them hard to fathom. Without an ideal of accuracy to work toward, no conversation can get started over how to work toward that ideal. The price of the postmodern emphasis on individuality, originality, and freedom from any intellectual constraint is isolation.

I should point out that thinkers of the modern era tried a compromise, attempting to achieve community without authority. Moderns allowed individuals to be their own authority and relied on a commonly distributed reason (or in Luther's case, the common endowment of the Holy Spirit in all Christians) to guarantee common interpretations. The attempt at compromise failed: during the modern period, Protestantism fragmented into hundreds of different sects, mostly on the basis of different interpretations of scripture.

Two considerations incline me to sympathize with the premodern church when it comes to biblical interpretation. The first is a concern for the unity of the church. The Gospel of John records Jesus's prayer for all believers, "that they all may be one,"[4] but this prayer has gone unanswered for a long time. All Christians hold the Bible as an important resource for the faith. But both the actual events of history and the logic behind those events that I have been trying to explain demonstrate that as commonly acknowledged authority to interpret the Bible goes, so goes Christian unity. When Christians began to group themselves under conflicting authorities during the Reformation (or even earlier, in conflicts with heretical movements and between what became the Roman Catholic and the Orthodox churches), the church fragmented. Conversely, I believe, the church will be unified again when her conflict over interpretive authority is resolved. Just how to resolve this conflict I do not know, and the whole topic raises difficult questions that run far beyond the scope of this book. But if, with Jesus, we pray for Christian unity, we must eventually abandon the modern and postmodern principle that each person's ability to understand the scriptures is as good as every other person's.

The second point has to do with the relationship between Christian character and the interpretation of scripture. For postmoderns, the worldview of the reader—her allegiance to feminism, or the Republican Party, or whatever—drives her interpretation of the text. For premoderns, on the other hand, the goal at least was for the biblical text to shape the worldview of the reader. The major question between these views, for a faithful Christian, is whether God expects the Bible to transform us, and the answer to that question is, I think, an obvious "yes." To put it another way, suppose it is true, as I have argued, that a reader's worldview always shapes the way she reads a text (so that modernism is excluded) and yet that some worldviews are more desirable, because more Christian, than others (so that postmodernism is excluded). Then something like the premodern approach to interpreting scripture—an approach whose key feature, for most people, is the search for someone wiser than themselves to help them understand what the Bible means and means for them—may be the way forward for the church in the twenty-first century.

Literalism

The modern appeal to reason alone had an important consequence that we have not yet discussed. In the premodern world of biblical interpretation, scripture was generally acknowledged to have multiple levels of meaning. In addition to the literal or historical sense—that is, the plain sense of the passage—interpreters found in the Bible one or more spiritual senses. For example, the story of Exodus was read not only as an account of the Hebrews' exit from Egypt but also as an allegory of redemption. Some of these allegories could be quite elaborate. In the allegory of the exodus, for instance, Moses stood for Christ, the Hebrew people for the church, the exodus for salvation, slavery in Egypt for bondage in sin, Pharaoh for Satan, the Red Sea for death, and the Promised Land for heaven.

It was also acknowledged, early on, that some passages of scripture might not be true in the literal sense but only in their spiritual senses. In some cases, the literal sense of a passage is so preposterous that anyone can see that some other sense is intended. When a ten-horned, seven-headed beast comes out of the sea in Revelation 13, for instance, or when Isaiah 55 prophesies that the trees will clap their hands, no one imagines that these are literal descriptions of future events. The early church fathers, however, took the principle beyond these entirely obvious cases. Augustine, for example, along with several others, considered the creation narrative of Genesis 1 to be true mostly in a spiritual sense.

That passage, according to Augustine, teaches principles like the sovereignty of God over creation and the goodness of the created world; questions about the length of time creation took, or the biological processes involved, he finds entirely uninteresting.

The modern period saw an increased emphasis on the literal sense of scripture, however, for several reasons. To begin with, spiritual senses are not the sort of meanings that modern methods of interpretation are designed to uncover—"to admit nothing as [the Bible's] teaching which did not most clearly derive from it" is a recipe for seeing only the literal sense of the scriptures. Yet the allegorical method of interpretation also lends itself to abuse—it's very easy to invent allegorical meanings for nearly anything. When too many baroque and conflicting allegorical interpretations arose, many interpreters abandoned the spiritual senses of scripture altogether. Finally, the literal sense of a text represents, so to speak, the lowest common denominator of interpretation, the sense that practically anyone can understand. As the modern era wore on and ordinary individuals became more comfortable interpreting the Bible for themselves, the literal sense gained in importance, since that tended to be the simplest level of interpretation. Taken to its logical conclusion, the modern interpretive stance results in a reader always understanding the Bible literally, except in those rare cases, like Revelation 13 or Isaiah 55, where some other level of meaning is forced upon him.

Many of my readers will recognize this stance—that the Bible should always be interpreted literally unless that interpretation is clearly unreasonable—as their own, or as one they have been taught. (In fact, it's exactly the principle of interpretation I was taught as a teenager.) But we should realize, now, that this stance is not simply a product of sincere Christian faith, but a product of sincere Christian faith combined with a modern worldview. Rethinking this modern worldview opens up many possibilities: I can remember the distinct relief I felt when it occurred to me, for the first time, that the early chapters of Genesis might be true on a symbolic level even if their literal, historical sense was, strictly speaking, false.

Yet this attitude can appear dangerous as well, because it opens up another possibility—that the entire Bible might be interpreted on a spiritual rather than a literal level. Why not read it like Aesop's fables, as a powerful collection of stories, poems, and other writings, where the question of literal truth simply doesn't arise? Many postmoderns are willing to take just this approach. They deny, or remain agnostic about, the historical truth of events like the calling of Abraham, the exodus from Egypt, and the resurrection of Jesus. But reading the Bible like a longer, more elaborate version of Aesop would cripple serious Christian faith—it shouldn't even be a possibility. So let's ask: why is it so important that the Bible be (literally, historically) *true*, rather than merely instructive or edifying or inspirational?

The answer, I suggest, is that the Bible is fundamentally the record of God's action in history. It begins with God initiating history in creation; it continues with God's calling Abraham and forming a special people, the nation of Israel. It passes to the life of a genuine historical man who was also God and to the founding of a uniquely inspired institution, the Christian church. It ends with the promise of a future divine intervention in history, a final judgment. The message of the long trajectory of the salvation story is that God acts in this world for purposes of judgment and redemption.[5] He has in the past with others; he will in the present and future with you. That's the story's point, and it isn't a very plausible point if the story isn't basically—literally, historically—true.

The basic reliability of the literal sense of scripture, then, should not be in question for a Christian. But the literal truth of the scriptures is not an end in itself; it serves the larger purpose of bringing people to trust in a God who acts. We should keep this in mind when questions about the historical accuracy of a Bible passage arise—what do we need to insist upon to maintain the integrity of the basic biblical message, and where can we be flexible? That God created the universe and everything in it is, I think, nonnegotiable. That this creation took exactly six twenty-four-hour days strikes me as a point not worth insisting on.

For Further Thought

1. What are the purposes of an education? Rank them in order from most important to least important.
2. What does it mean to love God with all your mind? Can you give examples of people who have done this, or activities that would amount to doing it?
3. Would it bother you if you were not allowed to interpret the Bible for yourself, for instance if your access to a Bible were physically restricted? Why or why not?
4. Consider the quote from Spinoza in this chapter. Is it a laudable ideal? A project doomed to failure? A demonstration of amazing arrogance? Should a contemporary biblical scholar take the same attitude or a different one?
5. Do some research on another denomination with an eye to figuring out what the theological differences are between your denomination and that one. How does each side appeal to the Bible? What might resolve the conflict of interpretations?

Culture and Irony

A central feature of postmodernity is the breakdown of cultural traditions all over the world. One anecdote captures the postmodern situation perfectly. A man was traveling in Japan at a time when the Japanese were showing a lively interest in the Western holiday of Christmas. Entering a shopping mall, he saw . . . Santa Claus on a cross!

The cultural changes flooding the world today range from large ones, like changing structures of marriage and childrearing and dissolving religious and ethnic barriers, to small ones, like eating different kinds of foods prepared in different ways. These changes result from other aspects of postmodernity, and they eventuate in distinctly postmodern attitudes.

The Times, They Are a-Changin'

The United States may be the most volatile culture in the world. We can see its culture changing in many ways. Marriage ceremonies, for instance, are less scripted than they used to be: more people write their own vows, get married in unusual locations, or don't bother to get married at all.

On television the other night I saw a program that followed the wedding of a black Baptist Southerner to a white Jewish New Yorker; the wedding contained Christian and Jewish elements, with a few Native American touches thrown in for flavor. Such a combination of races and of religions would have been unthinkable two generations ago.

Gender roles and sexual stereotypes have altered as well. No longer is the husband assumed to be the breadwinner of the family, and wives stay home increasingly rarely. Girls can wrestle and play football in high schools. Homosexual relationships receive more recognition in our society, and although gay people used to be denied national security clearances on the grounds that they could be blackmailed, this is no longer the case.

My supermarket carries mangoes from Mexico, kiwi fruit from New Zealand, and salmon from Chile or Norway. In addition to McDonalds or Kentucky Fried Chicken, I can get my lunch at Taco Bell. Besides traditional cookbooks like *The Joy of Cooking,* I have guides to Asian cuisine; using soy sauce in a dish long ago ceased to be remarkable. It is sometimes hard to remember that these are innovations; my parents (much less my grandparents!) never had them at my age.

That is just a sample. No doubt if you look around carefully, you can find many other instances of change from traditional ways of doing things. These are all alterations in the culture.

These sorts of changes, which are actually happening worldwide, can be thought of as one more way in which traditional authority is breaking down in the postmodern era. Remember, cultural traditions are instructions for living: when we violate them, for instance by not having a Christmas tree or by serving pie at a birthday party, it can feel somehow *wrong*. We have seen other aspects of this breakdown already: the refusal to credit traditional schemes of morality, older notions of the self, or ordinary ways of interpreting texts. In all of these respects, postmodernism is merely furthering the modern project in a more radical way. Modernism was all about questioning traditional sources of authority: the king, the church, the Bible, the ancient Greek and Roman sages. Certain aspects of its reliance on reason, however, combined with its implicit belief in the basic superiority of European culture, prevented it from questioning authority as far as it might have. On the fronts of ethics, self, interpretation, and cultural traditions, postmodernism is just finishing the job.

Roots of Cultural Change

There is a basic reason for cultural changes: they arise from increasing exposure to other cultures, that is, alternative ways of doing things. This exposure results in the recognition that the practices of any one culture are, for the most part, arbitrary; nothing written in the fabric of the universe says that brides have to wear white, or that a gold band on the left ring finger signals marriage, or that women but not men should wear skirts. These practices are all simply traditions, and once you come to see them that way, they are *merely* traditions—accidents of history that could have been otherwise if our ancestors had had a different aesthetic sense or lived in a different climate or been proselytized by a different religion.

In our time, the exposure to other cultures is a result of several different factors. The aftermath of colonialism, ironically, is one such factor: it was in the colonial era that white men traveled to all the far-flung cultures of the world and began the process of linking them together through ties of trade and government. Anthropology has made a point of studying these remote non-Western cultures and bringing home to us Westerners how different and yet how human they still are.

Other factors are economic. The world is now far more economically integrated than it has ever been in the past. Advances in technology and transport have made it feasible to distribute manufacturing around the world, to sell products far from where they are made, and to customize a single product for use in many different languages and cultures. For example, most of the clothing Americans wear is now made in the developing world, and many "American" cars are made from parts manufactured overseas.

The dramatically increasing power of telecommunications has been part of the global economic revolution, but it has also eroded the barriers between cultures. The Internet can connect any two points on the planet almost instantaneously. Furthermore, it allows people to broadcast their views to large, diverse audiences, the sort formerly available only to major networks. Satellite television allows footage produced on one side of the world to be received on the other. This state of affairs fulfills a prophecy that Marshall McLuhan made in the 1960s—that the world would become a "global village," with each part accessible to every other.

Alongside the flows of money, products, and information are flows of people. Between a half-million and a million people immigrate to the United States every year. Moreover, these immigrants are not primarily from the European nations that provided the first settlers: in 2000, the top ten points of origin for immigrants were Mexico, China, the Philippines, India, Vietnam, Nicaragua, El Salvador, Haiti, Cuba, and the Dominican Republic. These immigrants bring with them their own cuisines, their own religions, their own styles of family life. As they settle in the United States, often in large coastal cities but increasingly in the heartland as well, they transform the cultural landscape. When I lived outside of Washington, D.C., my apartment building (with twelve apartments) housed Vietnamese, Ethiopians, Chinese, and Mexicans, plus native-born whites and African Americans. In that kind of situation, it becomes impossible not to recognize the sheer contingency of any particular lifestyle: there but for mere chance, mere accidents of birth, go I.

Vertigo versus Mix 'n' Match

So much exposure to different cultures has a number of different psychological effects. One is a sort of cultural vertigo—a feeling that the ground is moving under your feet. What had seemed safe and reliable now often seems strange, even threatening. Since cultural change can feel threatening, it may provoke hostility. This feeling is most likely to occur to a modern; or we could say that, since this reaction is a matter of degree, your worldview is modern insofar as experiencing other cultures in your own backyard gives you vertigo. Celebrating a vegetarian Thanksgiving can give you this feeling; so can attending a Confucian wedding ceremony. And yet our society now contains a lot of vegetarians and Confucians, and there are likely to be more in the future, not fewer.

Vertigo has always been a product of exposure to other cultures. When ancient Athens became an empire and an international trading power, its citizens came into contact with Phoenicians, Egyptians, and Persians, not to mention other Greeks. This interaction ignited a debate about the true difference between "nature" and "custom" (the

ancient version of the genetics/environment distinction).
Many things that had before seemed part of the natural
order—beliefs in certain gods, slavery, the division between
Greeks and non-Greeks—now appeared merely customary,
hence relative and liable to change. Greeks of that era experienced the same sort of dislocation moderns feel today
when confronted with so many new cultural traditions and
the erosion of so many old ones.

A different reaction, more characteristic of postmoderns,
is to embrace change—in fact, to take an active role in it.
A postmodern is generally happy with the breakdown of
cultural traditions. The proliferation of choices may feel
freeing, the way that people from small towns often feel
freer when they move to the big city. Postmoderns are happy
to mix and match traditions, taking what seems appropriate
or interesting from various cultures and incorporating them
into a new style or synthesis. The Japanese decorator who
put Santa on the cross, for instance, was a paradigmatic
postmodern. A postmodern woman might wear Native
American jewelry, carry a Guatemalan purse, do yoga for
exercise, throw Cinco de Mayo parties, and study Chinese
cookery, all while working in a staid corporate law firm or
attending a traditional women's college. To the postmodern,
the traditions of the past are like a supply store, providing
off-the-shelf parts for a newly constructed identity.

This postmodern borrowing impulse is not confined
to teenagers, artists, or residents of New York City and
Los Angeles. Many individual Christians are "cafeteria
traditionalists," adhering to the parts of their inherited
faith they like and discarding uncomfortable teachings like
the doctrine of hell or the prohibition on premarital sex.
Christians also frequently borrow from other traditions of
Christianity, perhaps without realizing it. Many Protestants
celebrate Advent, which is one of six seasons observed in

the traditional liturgical calendar, without celebrating the seasons of Epiphany or Lent. Catholics borrow Protestant models of lay participation and Bible study. Traditional denominations draw on Pentecostal emphases on gifts of the Holy Spirit and enthusiasm in worship. Each of these innovations represents a cultural change, one often opposed by conservatives but embraced by others. The conservatives get vertigo; the embracers have a mix-and-match mentality.

Rootlessness

All this borrowing, stealing, adding, subtracting, grafting, and splicing of traditions leaves postmoderns without "roots" in the sense that anyone raised in a premodern culture might have had them. There is no all-embracing, unquestioned and unquestionable cultural envelope that keeps them secure in one way of doing things. They have traded roots for freedom and choice because, after all, deep roots keep you stuck in one place.

It's precisely this uprooted feeling, and the uprooting force of postmodernity generally, that feels threatening to someone raised with deeper roots. This isn't merely a matter of feeling comfortable with what's familiar—feeling uprooted is not like coming home to find your living room furniture rearranged. There's a much deeper source to the discontent.

Santa Claus *makes sense* in a children's story about the origin of Christmas gifts, with some admonitions to good behavior thrown in. He doesn't *belong* nailed to a cross: the cross is part of an entirely different story about the sinfulness of humanity and God's initiative in overcoming it. We may feel the same way when we see the cross used as jewelry by, say, Madonna, who isn't wearing it to

express her allegiance to that story of redemption. Devout
Hindus will feel this way when they see yoga used merely
for exercise rather than for spiritual enlightenment; Mexicans will feel this way when a Cinco de Mayo party has no
connection with Mexican independence; Catholics feel this
way when they see Advent and Christmas, the seasons of
awaiting and arrival, not followed by Epiphany and Lent,
the seasons of revelation and repentance.

Most traditions of any depth or consequence are like this:
they have their place in a broader context, a bigger story
that makes sense of a large chunk of life. Postmoderns, in
adapting bits and pieces of many traditions according to
their own lights, lose the sense of loyalty to something larger
that these traditions produced in their original holistic form.
In adapting elements of tradition for their own purposes,
detaching them from the larger story of which they are a
part, postmoderns treat symbols with less reverence than
others do. It doesn't matter to them that Santa is not surrounded by reindeer and elves, and it doesn't matter that
the cross isn't associated with redemption, resurrection,
and worship. This is not so bad when it comes to Santa,
but it's much more serious when it comes to the cross. In
losing the reverential attitude toward cultural symbols,
postmoderns have lost the sense of meaning those symbols
bring. That prevents them from sinking roots, and it can
threaten others' sense of meaning too.

Irony

At some level, postmoderns know about their rootlessness. It gives many of them a nagging angst. Many postmoderns carry the sense that, in refusing to acknowledge
anything fixed, larger than themselves, to which they are

accountable, they have lost touch with something important. This rootlessness produces a second attitude, however, marking their interactions with traditions: irony.

By irony I don't mean anything like sarcasm. Rather, irony is the postmodern awareness that, in a world of many incompatible traditions and cultures and religions, any choice among them is somewhat arbitrary. No single set of moral beliefs, no single political agenda, no single religion (much less a single nation, style of dress, cuisine, or set of holiday customs) is so obviously superior to others that it commands everyone's allegiance. People choose what they do because of when and where they were raised; their allegiances are due to their culture and history. Postmoderns know this is true of others, and they know it is true of themselves. Irony is a form of self-awareness.

Moderns and premoderns don't have this view of themselves. A modern thinks that most questions—and all the important ones—have right answers, and that we can find, or at least approach, those answers through the use of reason. Diversity on the large questions of life is due to the lack of reason in so many other people (or perhaps, if he is feeling modest, in himself). Premoderns typically weren't (or aren't—there are still premodern worldviews around today, even in America) exposed to other perspectives on the world, so questions about competing worldviews don't arise. The premodern atmosphere is complete; it has all the right answers already worked out, handed down by tradition and authority.

Neither the premodern nor the modern has the ironic sense of himself as a creature molded by the chances of time and place. The postmodern can't escape it. Postmoderns are inevitably sophisticated, at least in a certain way, due to their multicultural environment. They've seen too many competing traditions, been exposed to too many different streams of culture, seen too many critiques and unserious treatments of *everything,* for anything to seem obvious or clearly correct anymore. It's this skepticism, plus the loss of faith in reason as a standard for better and worse, that leads to the postmodern's ironic stance.

Postmodernism in the Arts

The characteristics of postmodern culture I have been discussing—the blending of different traditions, and relatedly, rootlessness and ironic detachment—are also characteristic of the fine arts in the postmodern era. To see how it got that way, we'll take an all-too-brief historical tour of artistic work.

In the premodern era, there was no such thing as a CD collection or an art museum. Someone always commissioned fine art—painting, music, theater, sculpture in wood or stone, architecture, and more—for some purpose. Greek playwrights wrote for festivals of Dionysus, medieval architects and stonemasons constructed venues for worshiping God, and painters painted and musicians composed for the benefit of wealthy patrons. Consequently, artists were viewed, and viewed themselves, as contributors to some larger project. The artist was not the main attraction, so we have comparatively little knowledge of the artists of premodernity. The painters and stonemasons and woodcarvers, the musicians and architects, are largely lost to us.

The modern period, with its new individualistic emphasis, saw a different attitude toward the artist. Artists were conceived of as geniuses, individuals blessed with rare gifts for producing original works. Mere exposure to the products of such a genius was an elevating experience. Fine art was no longer principally an adornment to some other religious or civic or domestic activity. It was this era that saw the emergence of "name" artists in a big way. Later, galleries and museums appeared. Art had become its own world, its own business, and with the slogan "art for art's sake" (unthinkable in a premodern context), its own end.

This collection of attitudes toward artists and art—thinking of artists as geniuses of originality, and art as its own privileged cultural sphere—predictably fostered a certain highbrow self-importance among artists and other members of the "art world." Postmodern art and artists are a reaction to the modern art scene.

Postmodern artists reject the emphasis on originality, and with it the idea of artistic genius, that the modern era promoted. In postmodern art, creativity lies not in coming up with a brand new idea, but in coming up with a new synthesis of old ideas. The old ideas are often treated not respectfully but whimsically. You can see this pattern in contemporary electronic music, which is often a collection of short samples from other artists' works, rearranged and modified to create an entirely new sound. Often the sampled music is deliberately out of place or even corny—my favorite in this genre is an album consisting of hip-hop remixes of Lawrence Welk tunes. Fashion is an easy place to spot the postmodern influence: when fashions from the 1970s are re-run by Madison Avenue today, part of the appeal is the "retro" look, whereas in the 1970s those fashions were just cool. Postmodern architecture incorporates a mélange of styles into a single building, each element divorced from its historical context. But even blueprints can be done ironically: the Sony building in New York looks like a Chippendale cabinet against the skyline. A less playful, more caustic example of ironic detachment is a series of black and white photographs that artist Cindy Sherman took in the 1970s. Each photograph showcases herself in a pose, costume, and setting that could be from any of a hundred movies: the vulnerable naïf in the big city, the housewife mopping the floor, the lonely single woman staring out the window, the seductress, the damsel in distress, and so on. In these photos Sherman draws attention to the constructed roles our society, and especially its films, has for women, and to the fact that, far from being seen as a unique individual, she can fill any one of them.

In selecting and rearranging old works to create their own new ones, postmodern artists exemplify the mix-and-match mentality I discussed earlier. In doing so, they set themselves apart from the modern emphasis on original artistry. However, postmodern artists don't align themselves with any tradition or larger project either, as a premodern would have. Their natural environment is still the art world of galleries and museums, even if they view these institutions cynically sometimes. Their artworks juxtapose and contextualize the older elements they use in ways that, on the one hand, emphasize their historical influences and social construction, but on the other hand, refuse to embrace and be part of any tradition of music or film or design. Rather, these postmodern works are parasitic on tradition: commenting on it, borrowing from it, but not contributing to it.

Ironic Faith?

We need to return to the role of irony in the postmodern consciousness, because it has some important effects that I haven't yet mentioned. The global exposure and competing traditions that undermine certainty in every other realm for a postmodern also undermine moral and religious certainty. Thus, postmoderns are ironic about their moral commitments. Many postmoderns have passionate ethical convictions—for instance, about the importance of tolerance and the need to respect other cultures. At the same time, a genuine postmodern knows that these convictions are shared by hardly any other culture in the world, and she knows that she cannot persuade everyone to her view. Her own ethical convictions are the result of her own cultural and historical placement. Aware of this, she nevertheless maintains them, but without the innocent belief that her convictions are obvious to any thinking person.

Something like this also applies to postmodern Christians who have been affected by critical scholarship on the Bible or philosophical arguments against the existence of God, or who have had striking, positive experiences with devotees of other religions. Many conservative Christians are modern in their outlook: they believe that reason shows Christianity to be clearly superior to other faiths. Thus Bill Bright, founder of Campus Crusade, writes,

> [T]he evidence confirming the deity of the Lord Jesus Christ
> is overwhelmingly conclusive to any honest, objective seeker
> after truth.[1]

For a postmodern, however, this old assumption—that Christianity is somehow obviously, unquestionably the true faith and that anyone who denies it is dishonest or stupid or both—is gone. The exposure to alternative perspectives—and the ability to see them as genuine alternatives—has ended it. Seeing that alternatives to Christianity are neither intellectually unfounded nor morally bankrupt, she may all the same decide to commit to the Christian life. She can still believe, though not with the unselfconscious ease she had before. Faith now comes with a touch of irony. It is seen, very clearly, as the *gift* of God.

To a modern or premodern, it's tempting to think that ironic faith isn't really faith, nor are ironic ethics really ethics. But that would be a mistake. What the postmodern doesn't have is innocent, unselfconscious, and therefore self-confident faith or ethics. I think Peter, in the last chapter of John's Gospel, evinces something like the ironic attitude (though, to be sure, Peter was no postmodern). Twice Jesus asks whether Peter "truly loves" him. Before the crucifixion, Peter would certainly have answered yes. Now, however, having denied his Master three times, Peter won't take the bait. "Lord, you know that I love you," he answers. Not "I truly love you"; he has lost his old confidence in himself. He is aware that his love for Jesus will break, given circumstances beyond his control. But this honest, self-aware answer is enough for Jesus. He says to Peter, "Follow me!" and Peter goes on to become the head of the church.

For Further Thought

1. Make a list of the ways you are connected to other countries in the world—by the food you buy, the clothes you wear, the car you drive, the news you get, and so on. Then try to make a list of the connections your parents would have had at your age. Then for, say, a peasant at the time of the Reformation.

2. Is it important to you that the practices of your church or denomination stay the same? Why or why not?

3. Find examples in television shows or movies of self-aware irony. Those examples would not have been present a generation ago; why are they there now?

4. Under what circumstances would you be willing to change your citizenship? Under what circum-

stances would you be willing to change your religious affiliation?

5. People have been willing to die for their country and for their religion. Do you think a postmodern would be willing to become a martyr?

6. Is it possible to be genuinely ironic *and* committed in areas like morality or religious faith? Explore this.

History and Hope

The Functions of History

Why do we bother studying history?

At least three reasons have been put forward. First, across all times and cultures, people have looked for practical lessons in the course of history. Usually, they have thought they could find some reliable lessons there: the past teaches the consequences of right and wrong actions, the fortunes that attend strong and weak characters, and the principles of success and failure. The earliest historical accounts we have are clearly intended to teach us something. In his *Histories,* Herodotus, the "father of history," tells how a handful of free, self-reliant Greek city-states banded together and defeated the prideful, autocratic Persian empire. Whoever compiled the historical books of the Old Testament relates the rise, fall, and partial restoration of the nation of Israel. Both authors intended their lessons to apply to future readers: Herodotus's book is a brief for free government and humble rulers; the Old Testament is testimony to the faithfulness of God toward an often-rebellious people, even (or especially) when that faithfulness is hard for human eyes to detect.

Besides supplying moral examples and lessons for future generations, history also shapes the identity of a people. The citizens of Athens, Sparta, and the other city-states who fought against Persia learned to think of themselves as "Greeks" in part by sharing the tales that Herodotus collected, and ancient Israel was forged into a nation in part by remembering the exodus, the time in the wilderness, and the conquest and settling of their land. These kinds of historical narratives help determine what is meant by "we": "we Greeks" fought Persia; "we Israelites" were enslaved in Egypt. Likewise, "we Americans" rebelled against the British and fought for independence. These "we" statements continue to influence the way people think of themselves even if they or their parents are immigrants to Greece or Israel or America and their biological ancestors had nothing to do with the historical events in question.

Finally, history is sometimes recruited to do more than supply life lessons from the past or provide founding narratives for a nation or culture. Many people have looked for a deeper trajectory to history: a moral pattern that could be projected into the future, some promise or guarantee that eventually justice would be done, truth would triumph, and the world would be put right. This kind of "end-times" belief, by no means confined to Christianity, is also a purpose of the study of history.

Premodern individuals found it easy to embrace these functions of history. The practical and moral lessons embodied in stories of heroes and villains were clear enough; the "founding narratives"—stories about how a nation or people originated—set the tone for a whole premodern culture. The great monotheistic religions, all of which originated in premodernity, also found it easy to teach that someday the whole world would be put right. Precisely because history has these deep practical consequences, however, it is susceptible to bias and partiality. Founding narratives conflict; stories of the past can be told in different ways. To address these problems, historians in the modern period aimed for "objectivity," which in practice meant that while history still had meaning, it didn't wear it on its sleeve. Postmoderns, on the other hand, have given up trying to find clear practical lessons, or national identities, or future hopes, through the study of history. Losing these dimensions of historical meaning makes postmodernism profoundly different from the worldviews that came before it.

Lessons from the Past

An absence of skepticism about history marks premodernism. The premodern mind trusts that stories of the past are reasonably accurate. The lessons those stories impart are known and studied; often figures of history are held up as ideals. I emphasize that this trait belongs to premodern*ism*, the mind-set, not premodern*ity*, the historical period, because Herodotus certainly has a (somewhat) critical attitude toward accounts of the past, while many contemporary people do not.

To illustrate, I'll begin with an example that many of my readers will be familiar with: the settling of the North American continent. A very short version of the canonical story, which many of us have in our heads as a thumbnail sketch of American history, goes something like this:

People came to America from Europe for religious and political freedom and in search of a better life. They wanted to run their own lives in a new country. They established colonies on the Atlantic seacoast, which with hard work eventually succeeded. Gradually more people came, and as the eastern part of the country filled up, pioneers pushed westward across the Appalachians, turning wilderness into farms. More settlers headed into the central plains, raising cattle and wheat. Others journeyed all the way to California, so that eventually the United States stretched from coast to coast.

You know how to fill in the details. Some of the lessons derived from this history are that freedom and respect for the individual are precious American birthrights; that hard work eventually pays off; that the spirit of rugged individualism overcomes all kinds of obstacles; that the prosperity and power of the United States derive from the independence and industry of her citizens. The identity of Americans, shaped by this story, is of a plucky, independent people who exercised initiative and carved out new lives for themselves against significant odds. (The American identity, according to this story, is also heavily European in origin.) Some have projected this story into the future: America's ideals of democracy and freedom are a beacon to the world, leading to a better life for all nations, once they reform on the American model.

Taken baldly, at simple face value, that is a premodernist account of American history. It is premodernist because it is uncritical, or unskeptical: it does not contain, or respond to, alternative perspectives on the events it relates. Because history has the functions it has—supplying practical lessons and moral examples, shaping a culture's identity and even influencing one's view of destiny—it is no surprise that a culture's history of itself will be somewhat self-serving, casting itself in the role of good guy, emphasizing its virtues and minimizing its shortcomings. The canonical American history we just skimmed over does this: the American character, according to it, is one of freedom-loving, pioneering, rugged individualism. This conception of our own history has a great deal of influence on how Americans think of themselves. The pattern, however, with various cultural adaptations, is virtually universal: it is the pattern of the British version of British history, the Arab version of Arab history, the Chinese version of Chinese history, and so on. It takes alternate perspectives—the Jewish version of Arab history, the Korean version of Chinese history, the Indian version of British history—to shed the blinders of a too-trusting premodernist mind-set.

Let's go back to our American history example. The same set of events looks very different if you are a Native American. Then each advance of European civilization is a retreat for your own; in telling the history of the times, you dwell on how your people were devastated by disease, tricked into signing one-sided agreements, forced out of their ancestral lands by violence, and had treaties and guarantees constantly broken by land-hungry, Indian-hating whites. The history looks different still if you are an African-American. In that case, whatever else you say, you mention how white people, who spoke so readily of freedom and enshrined the noble notion of human rights in their Declaration of Independence, kept your ancestors as chattel and enshrined the institution of slavery in their Constitution. The same history looks different still if you are a Mexican: the Spanish settlement of Mexico comes into the foreground, while the Anglo settlement of the rest of North America is relatively unimportant—except, of course, for the part where the Anglos take half of your land, from Texas to California, for their own territory. The history even looks different if your ancestors came from Georgia (the canonical story tilts toward Pilgrims and Puritans, settlers in New England). Since Georgia began as a penal colony, "freedom" takes on an ironic twist as the motive for settlement. French Canadians, Puerto Ricans, and Asian immigrants to the West Coast (or their descendants) will all tell the history of the settling of North America in many different ways, from different perspectives, with different emphases.

So which account is genuine? Which is the real history? The first logical thought is that all of these different narratives can be genuine historical accounts. And certainly, if we could get representatives from all these different groups in a room, they could all agree that no one had invented any historical events. That, however, is a far cry from accepting another person's draft of history. The trouble is that the different drafts offer different, sometimes incompatible lessons: are freedom and individual rights foundation stones of the American experience, or are they fig leaves covering darker motives? Is it hard work, or theft, that eventually pays off? You may be familiar with similar debates: is it America's Christian origins, or her tradition of religious tolerance, that is responsible for her moral strength? The same kinds of questions arise regarding how Americans are to think of themselves: are "we" European in origin? Were "we" ever enslaved, or discriminated against, in this country? Did "we" acquire land, or lose it, during the course of American history? With too many competing versions of history, we lose the ability to learn from it, or more generally, to put it to the practical ends that make history interesting and powerful in the first place.

Premodern views of history don't suffer from this cacophony of rival voices or tolerate it. Either a premodern culture is insulated from other cultures and thus from other versions of history, or one cultural strand is so dominant that it drowns out other interpretations.

Modernism, however, does have the problem of multiple versions of history. Sometime in the modern period, it became both clear and problematic that history could be slanted for propaganda purposes. Because it was such a polarizing event, the French Revolution was a turning point in this regard. About it, Friedrich Nietzsche wrote:

> [N]oble and enthusiastic spectators from all over Europe contemplated it from a distance and interpreted it according to their own indignations and enthusiasms for so long, and so passionately, that the text finally disappeared under the interpretation. . . .[1]

To surmount this problem, moderns sought to turn history into a science and an academic discipline. History was to be told from an objective, neutral standpoint—the standpoint of reason. The job of the historian was simply to tell it "how it really was," not to advance any particular agenda. History produced in this way was to be history for all humanity, a tale of the past that any human being could accept and endorse. This kind of history would get beyond the partial perspectives that bedeviled premodern historical accounts. Whatever moral lessons emerged from a historical narrative produced in this fashion should command consensus from all parties, because the professional, scientific historian had simply told events the way they happened. The facts would speak for themselves.

Doubtful Lessons

Postmoderns have lost faith in this ideal of neutral, objective history. Their critique goes something like this: the point of producing an objective history is to reconcile opposing accounts—"opposing" in the sense that the different versions support different lessons and evaluations and identities, not in the sense that one version describes an event that the other denies ever happened. In other words, the modern historian is not merely trying to eliminate *falsity* from his account of history—presumably that's not too hard—but he's also trying to eliminate something much subtler, namely, *prejudice* or *partiality.*

Is this really possible? Postmoderns don't think so, and they draw this conclusion from looking at the substantive historical accounts that modernism has produced. Every account of history is related from some perspective; it is always geared to some audience or another; it emphasizes some events at the expense of others. No account of history is perfectly fair to everyone concerned—not because historians are bigots, but simply because what's interesting and important to one set of people is not always interesting or important to everyone else. A historical account has to have a narrative thread, and maintaining that thread requires taking one point of view rather than another, playing up one set of historical connections while sidelining others. Since doing history always involves a selection of some facts rather than others, emphasizing some facts over others, connecting some facts rather than others, the facts never "speak for themselves." There's always a historian arranging the facts, determining (perhaps within some limits) what they say.

To illustrate the postmodern perspective on history, think of how people answer the question, "Why did John and Jane get divorced?" (Pick your own John and Jane—it helps the example if the divorce is bitter.) Usually everyone can agree on what happened, at a bare, uninteresting level: whether Jane had an affair or whether John consumed alcohol. But the explanation for the divorce is likely to be rather different, depending on who you talk to. John's friends are likely to offer one interpretation, and Jane's friends will offer another, incompatible one. Again, these accounts will not be incompatible in that one side asserts what the other one denies—for instance, they will not disagree on whether John ever slapped Jane, or vice versa—at least, there doesn't have to be any disagreement of that kind. The incompatibility of the interpretations lies in the account of what caused what, which events were important, which actions were justified, and so on. The more bitter and contested the divorce, the farther the competing accounts are likely to diverge and the harder it will be for a third party to understand what really happened—if it makes sense to speak of "what really happened."

The world is full of failed marriages, bitter divorces, and half-hearted reconciliations, not only among individuals but among peoples as well. Native Americans, European settlers, and African slaves—or more properly, the descendants of all these groups—form one complicated family tangle. Anyone with a knowledge of world history can easily come up with other examples: Greeks and Turks, Turks and Armenians, Armenians and Azerbaijanis, Arabs and Jews, Jews and Germans, Germans and French, French and English, English and Irish . . . the list goes on for a very, very long time. In such a climate it's no wonder that the modern ideal of neutral history is impossible to achieve.

Perhaps the example of John and Jane illustrates the poverty of the idea that history should contain "just the facts." What this suggestion amounts to in actual practice is that a historical account should contain only the parts that everyone can agree on (the "facts") and leave out the parts that people disagree about ("interpretations"). This gets us nowhere, however. People don't produce divergent accounts of history because they lie or because they haven't done enough research. More precisely, mere falsehoods are fairly easily corrected. People produce divergent accounts because they emphasize different facts, relate them differently, and draw different patterns among them.

If there are competing versions of history, what determines which version is eventually accepted? The modern has faith that "the truth will out": that what's eventually accepted is the *right* version. This is, indeed, a matter of faith; in fact, it is one of modernism's eschatological hopes, something I will discuss presently. The postmodern doesn't have this faith. For her, which version gets accepted, either now or in the future, is simply a matter of power. In other words, the vagaries of time allow one group or another to get an upper hand. At that point they are in a position to force their version of history onto others and to suppress alternative accounts. This imposition rarely involves any actual violence; rather, it occurs as a result of what people in positions of influence decide. That is why, for instance, the history of white people in North America was once told largely as the story of intrepid pioneers, and not as the story of genocidal land-thieves. For a postmodern, the only reliable thing to say is that the winners write history.

Authority and History

Because postmoderns are convinced that there is no such thing as history without partiality, the claims of modern-minded historians (or more frequently, modern-minded laypeople who admire particular historians) to have produced impartial history ring worse than false. They sound sinister to a postmodern. For it is not as if people have stopped trying to learn lessons from history. Nor have people stopped making moral judgments about the actors in history. Nor, finally, have people somehow shuffled off the influence that historical narratives exert on how they conceive of themselves. On the contrary, these ethical elements of history are alive and well. The ideal of impartial history gives these ethical lessons and judgments and identities an aura of objectivity. It allows one to say, "These are the *real* lessons you should take to heart; these are the *real* heroes of history; these are the *real* villains; this is who you *really* are; this is what this country is *really* about," and so on. And if you had an agenda to push, there would be no better way to push it than to slant history your way, then publish it as something objective and neutral. The modern claim to tell objective history is, for the postmodern, a too-convenient mask for the exercise of power.

To put it in terms used earlier, at issue is a form of authority: authority over how the past is related, authority to determine which version of events counts as true and accurate. This authority has important ethical ramifications: it identifies heroes and villains, national characters, historical trends, and cherished public values. Like all forms of authority, it can be and has been abused. The most common abuse encourages jingoistic forms of patriotism, but historical authority can also be used to demonize a culture. Rather than permit historical authority to be abused, postmodernism destroys it. Postmoderns do not acknowledge any authoritative version of history. Rather, they insist, all historical narratives are inevitably biased in one direction or another, intentionally or not. Consequently, there is no version of history that you *must* listen to: you don't have to take your cues from anyone.

In summary, premoderns didn't question the authority of traditional stories of the past. Moderns questioned them but tried to find the true (objective, absolute) rendition of the past through the scientific historian's use of reason and evidence. Postmoderns have abandoned the idea of an authoritative version of history altogether.

Metanarratives, Premodern and Modern

I've focused on how people draw practical lessons from history and how they learn from historical narratives to think of themselves and the groups of which they are a part. It's possible, however, to think more broadly and to view all of history as one giant moral drama. Anyone who thinks like this believes that, in one way or another, the world is advancing through time to a climax; that history is not, at the cosmic level, just "one damned thing after another." Postmoderns call these visions "metanarratives"—big, overarching stories that explain and justify and place in context the other smaller stories that make up most historical writing.

The premodern mind looked at history through a religious lens. In the Judeo-Christian tradition, part of that religious worldview was a vision of history as an arc beginning with humanity's creation in fellowship with God, continuing through a fall away from God and the experience of suffering and redemption, and finally, in the future, culminating in a judgment and restoration to fellowship with God for the righteous. This is the Judeo-Christian metanarrative. Obviously it has different versions in Judaism and Christianity and even further variations within their different branches. As a metanarrative, however, it applies to all of history. What happens early in the story—for example, whether an individual or nation embraces or rejects God and his ways—determines what happens later, namely, how that same individual or nation fares at the last judgment.

Metanarratives give meaning to individual events, tying them together in the broadest possible fashion. They help structure all of life around a pre-ordained trajectory of history. For Christians, this mechanism structures all of life around one's relationship with God after being saved through faith in Jesus Christ, anticipating the final restoration of fellowship with God that occurs only at the end of the world. Metanarratives also give hope, a precious commodity for human beings: no matter what suffering occurs in the present, it will all be made right (the metanarrative assures us) in the future. For history is trending toward justice, toward redemption, toward good things.

That, as I said, is more or less the premodern worldview, or anyway a very prominent strand of it, especially in Western civilization. (And it may be the granddaddy of all metanarratives: it is not clear that the ancient civilizations of Greece or India or China had anything like a metanarrative of history.) The Christian metanarrative was, of course, part of the Christian religion, which rested on the authority of the church and the Bible. When those authorities came under pressure during the Enlightenment, the Christian metanarrative lost followers. Modernism, however, offered a metanarrative of its own. We have already seen its substitute—hope in Progress. The application of reason to more and more areas of human life was supposed to lift human beings out of darkness, superstition, and backwardness. It was supposed to inevitably result in harmony, peace, and justice for all. That is a metanarrative just as surely as is the Christian one. The same elements are present: the life-structuring power of the big story, the guarantee of hope for the future, the comfort in present suffering through the promise of better things to come.

Modernism produced other metanarratives as well. I'll mention two, one passé and one current, just to sharpen the picture a bit. Communism had a metanarrative of history wherein humanity progressed through stages of economic development toward a final end. After an initial stage of hunting and gathering, humanity advanced to primitive agriculture, then developed the slave-based economies of the ancient world. These in turn evolved into medieval feudalism, which ultimately gave birth to the industrial capitalism of Marx's day. Humanity's progress would not stop there, however, prophesied Marx. After an (inevitable) worldwide workers' revolution, the dictatorship of the proletariat would emerge, followed by a utopian state of perfect justice and harmony. The reasons for war would dissolve, and each person would be at peace with his neighbor; wealth would come from each according to his ability and flow to each according to his need. This metanarrative is a promise of redemption just as surely as is the book of Revelation. It doesn't include any supernatural actors, but believing it does require an act of faith.

Another metanarrative, more common than the communist one these days, places its ultimate hope in the spread of democracy and free markets. Not everyone who supports democracy and free markets does so in the context of a metanarrative. Many people simply think that, whatever injustice and foolishness gets perpetrated in an election or a free exchange, it pales in comparison to the injustice and foolishness you could expect from more authoritarian methods of running the government or the economy. However, other supporters of democracy and capitalism are more hopeful. According to such partisans, votes and markets guarantee peace, harmony, and justice around the world: they play the role for some in the free world that the dictatorship of the proletariat did for communists. Some people go further and think democracy and free markets are *destined* to spread around the globe, due to the obvious (to them) lameness of every other political and economic model. At this point we're dealing with a full-fledged metanarrative: a big story that offers hope for the future and a promise that everything will be made right.

"Incredulity toward Metanarratives"

The word "metanarrative" was coined by Jean-Francois Lyotard in a book called *The Postmodern Condition,* written in 1979. In that book he provided one of the key definitions of postmodernism: "incredulity toward metanarratives." In other words, postmodernism, for Lyotard, was the intellectual state one had reached when one no longer believed *any* big story about history, whether religious or secular. Postmodernism involves the loss of any hope that some larger-than-human force—be it God or History or Progress or Science or Reason—is going to come to the aid of humanity and make everything all right in the end. Postmoderns believe that we make our own bed, historically speaking, and we have to lie in it; and that's all there is to say. Except, maybe, that we're not such good bed-makers.

The roots of this loss of hope should be familiar by now. One is simply that none of the great hopeful promises have panned out—the great redemption, however one understands it, always lies around the historical bend. Postmoderns have lost faith and given up hoping. The other principal source of "incredulity toward metanarratives" is the concern with power: metanarratives, like moral absolutes and historical accounts generally, establish winners and losers, good guys and bad guys, in the march of time. They divide people into Christians and non-Christians, or Muslims and non-Muslims, or progressives and reactionaries, or worker heroes and bourgeois oppressors, and so on. Embracing a metanarrative gives members of the favored group a license to feel and act superior to the members of the non-favored group. That's something postmoderns want to avoid.

Postmoderns themselves divide into various camps on the question of how history will pan out. Some are pessimists, who see little hope for humanity and conclude that all of its resources—religious traditions, scientific knowledge, the power of reason—are now proven inadequate and exhausted. Lyotard himself advocates innovation for the sake of innovation—the main thing is to keep discussion flowing and ideas unstable, though there is no particular destination or purpose to the whole endeavor. Others are optimists: there is no *guarantee* that humanity will work out all right—thus no metanarrative—but the future is what we make it, and the best we can do is work for peace and justice in the opportunities we find around us.

Christianity's Metanarrative

Some liberal Christians have thought we could do without the metanarrative element in Christianity. Specifically, they have denied that God will ultimately intervene in history to bring about "a new heaven and a new earth," or they have denied that each individual Christian could expect a resurrection to fellowship with God, or both. The general theme is that what God does is nothing over and above what we human beings do. I have thought about these claims (I used to be attracted to them) and concluded that the no-metanarrative brand of Christianity is not very appealing. Paul has it right: "If only for this life we have hope in Christ, we are to be pitied more than all men."[2]

Christianity is a religion of great hope. Yet for some reason, I can remember many sermons on faith and many on love, but I can't remember many on hope. Perhaps we do not dwell on distinctively Christian hope because we have bought in to modern promises: of increased leisure and wealth through technological progress, of longevity and health through medical advance, of peace through reasoned discussion, of security through retirement planning, of technology or the market or a political program saving us from the ills we fear. Postmodernism blows the whistle on the many false promises of modernity, which puts its faith in reason and progress rather than in God. Postmoderns are admirably clear-eyed about the failures of modernity and about the sickness, oppression, and death that pervade our world. Their multiple alternative accounts of history have the merit of bringing these evils to our attention. Postmodern thought, however, is critical, skeptical, and deconstructive, without any new remedies to offer. It often engenders a worldview of deep hopelessness.

In the face of this pessimism, however, Christianity offers not cheery optimism but divine promises. Things will not get better by themselves, Christianity tells us. But in the face of death, we have the promise of resurrection; in the face of illness and disability, we have the promise of redeemed bodies; in the face of environmental degradation caused by greed and carelessness, we have the promise of a creation freed from bondage; in the face of war, oppression, and social conflict, we have the promise of an eternal kingdom of peace. These promises are a Christian's hope. Relying on them is an alternative to both the rose-colored optimism of modernity and the caustic cynicism of postmodernity. In confronting postmodernism and in attempting to make Christianity attractive to postmodern people, a renewed emphasis on the hope we have in Christ might make a world of difference.

For Further Thought

1. Why do you think history is worth learning? (Or is it worth learning?)
2. Pick a historical event that has great meaning for you—perhaps the American Revolution or the Civil War. Then do some research to discover how "the other side" views this event.
3. Is it possible for history to lead to moral conclusions? Or is it just a sequence of events, meaningless in themselves?
4. Can a metanarrative be extracted from studying history, or do we need something like divine revelation?
5. Are any historical events tragic or ironic or inspiring in and of themselves? Or is that just a matter of how a historian tells the story?
6. Is it possible to tell the history of women in America, for example, from a neutral standpoint? What would objectivity on this subject be like?
7. Is it bias if history books only include the deeds of relatively famous and influential people? Or do they need to include the activities of obscure individuals?
8. History was originally included in school curricula in order to foster patriotism in young people. Is that a reasonable goal, or is it a recipe for intellectual blindness?

Epilogue

If you've made it this far, you now have a working knowledge of what postmodernism is. I don't know what reaction it has produced in you: you may be excited, frightened, bewildered, or maybe all three. You may feel that finally someone understands you. Or you may feel like you went to sleep and woke up to a strange and different world.

In this final chapter I'd like to help you grapple with the idea of a shift in worldview. First, I'll try to put the current shift, the turn toward postmodernism, into perspective. Once we see how this worldview shift is like some others in the past, we can ask more specific questions about the main intellectual task that postmodernism presents to us.

How Big a Deal is Postmodernism?

I have written an entire book on the postmodern worldview, and mine is certainly not the only one. Postmodernism is a big topic these days. It's worth asking, however, how big a topic it *deserves* to be, and this is a question that doesn't get asked very much. For those who choose to think about such things, worldview shifts can be a little heady, either extremely exciting or extremely disturbing. The excited tend to think postmodernism will change everything, Christianity included, forever; the disturbed can't wait for it to pass. I think both attitudes are wrong.

Postmodernism is a worldview shift; it is a wide-angle framework embracing many parts of life. It affects how a person thinks on many topics and on many levels. I hope by now you have some sense of that. It is not likely to be a flash in the pan, since it has emerged in response to the shortcomings of modernism. Therefore, modernism is not likely to make a return, at least not in its full-dress version. It has largely spent its force in Western civilization, I think, and while it retains great power in many areas of our culture, it's the power of inertia, not of vitality.

On the other hand, postmodernism itself may mutate. I have spoken in extremely general terms in this book about "modernism" and "premodernism," but really there are many different versions of modern and premodern worldviews. The modernism of the Enlightenment differs significantly from the modernism of the nineteenth century; it differs geographically too, for instance between France and Britain. So what now look like minor traits of postmodernism may come to be major elements of it, and what now look like structural timbers of the postmodern worldview may evolve into optional accessories.

At any rate, postmodernism is not the last worldview in history. To see this, it helps to realize how many times Christianity has had to change its relationship to the surrounding intellectual climate. For instance, sometime in the first or second century, Christians stopped thinking of themselves as a branch of Judaism, albeit one particularly welcoming to Gentiles, and started thinking of themselves as a new religion meant for every people, language, tribe, and nation on earth. That was quite a mental change, but Christianity survived and was stronger for it.

In A.D. 410 Rome was a major Christian center and the capital of an officially Christian empire. Many Christians thought of Roman civilization and Christian civilization as identical. Yet the barbarian Visigoths sacked the great city. Many Christians were devastated. Jerome, who translated the Bible into Latin, wrote, "My voice sticks in my throat; and, as I dictate, sobs choke my utterance. The City which had taken the whole world was itself taken." It took Augustine's massive book *City of God* to put things in a fresh perspective for Christians. That book argued, against the prevailing worldview, that Roman civilization had been built on pride and arrogance. Augustine emphasized that Christians have their true citizenship in heaven, not anywhere on earth.

To take another example, during the early Middle Ages Christian scholars enjoyed a fairly tidy intellectual world. The Bible was the principal authoritative text, but the writings of church fathers and some borrowings from Neoplatonic philosophy also played a role. Into this closed milieu, around 1250 or so, broke the works of Aristotle, newly available in Europe for the first time since antiquity. Aristotle had written on practically every topic under the sun: the motions of animals, the weather, the stars and planets, politics, ethics, logic, physics, the soul, and many others. His philosophical system explained much more about the world than any Christian scholar had ever hoped to, yet it had no room for a personal God who took an interest in his creatures. The universities of Europe were in turmoil: how should they handle this pagan body of knowledge, so rich and yet so dangerous? The giant intellect of Thomas Aquinas came to the church's rescue. In his enormous

Summa Theologiae, he outlined a profoundly Christian worldview that nevertheless incorporated a great deal of Aristotelian insight.

In the seventeenth century, Christians had to adapt to the intellectual world of the Enlightenment; and in the nineteenth century, to the intellectual world inaugurated by Darwin's theory of evolution. (That last transition was less smooth than some of the others.) At many times, in lots of ways, Christians have changed their worldviews in response to shifts in the surrounding culture. Each time, they succeeded in producing a new form of Christianity responsive to the times: under persecution from Rome, under the protection of Rome, or without Rome; ignorant of Aristotle, incorporating Aristotle, and after Aristotle became passé; under empire, monarchy, and democracy; before and after modern science; before and after the theory of evolution.

I mention all this history to give you a sense of perspective. As I argued in the first chapter, Christians have to draw on their surrounding culture for how to think about many aspects of life, since God has left us free in many areas. Consequently, as the tides of history rise and fall, worldviews rise and fall with them, including the worldviews of Christians. Christian intellectual change is not uncommon and should not be unexpected. (That is why there is such a thing as *a* Christian worldview, but no such thing as *the* Christian worldview.) This is part of living *in* the world.

Postmodernism, as outlined in this book, is the latest large-scale cultural change to hit Western civilization. It will change a lot of things for Christians and non-Christians alike. I don't know how long it will last—a decade, a generation, perhaps a century or two. Postmodernism may collapse from its own contradictions and its inability to account for historical events, the way certain aspects of modernism have. September 11, 2001, may do to postmodern moral relativism what the Holocaust did to modern ideas of moral progress. Alternatively, postmodernism may be sidelined into irrelevance, especially from a Christian point of view. By 2025, two-thirds of Christians will live in Latin America, Africa, and Asia, cultures where the history and guiding ideas of Western civilization—the springs of postmodern thought—are simply much less important than they are in North America and Europe.

It is a fairly safe bet that the general distrust of truth and knowledge that marks postmodernism is temporary. This skeptical syndrome flares up at intervals throughout history; it is a response to intellectual exhaustion and often portends something remarkable and new. It appeared in the ancient Mediterranean world when ancient philosophy had hardened into fruitless dickering between firmly established schools of thought. Some form of skepticism persisted as long as these philosophical schools persisted, which was more or less until the establishment of Christianity in the old Roman Empire. The syndrome appeared again in India at a time when Hindu philosophy was fragmenting and just before the Buddha launched his religious and philosophical revolution. Again, in Europe just prior to the modern era's burst of creativity, the exhaustion of premodern ways of thinking and the religious conflicts of the Reformation gave birth to a skeptical movement. Postmodern doubt is a frame of mind in the same mold, a response to the fruitlessness of modern approaches. Because a new way forward has always manifested itself before, we can expect that it will do so again. The shape of that intellectual revolution to come, however, is not yet clear.

Wherever the winds of intellectual change carry our civilization—and these things really cannot be predicted—the fact remains that postmodernism, unlike the universal church, is a human creation. Like all human creations, postmodernism will eventually crumble, while even the powers of hell cannot destroy the church.

The Fundamental Issue

Taking the long view gives one a sense of perspective. It can also induce a sense of complacency, however, and that is not something I mean to encourage. When Rome fell, Augustine spent more than a decade writing the book that would help Christians of his era grapple with the worldview shift that was upon them. Aquinas's *Summa,* his comprehensive response to the threat of Aristotelianism, was arguably the effort he spent his life preparing for. So as a new worldview penetrates our culture, we still are called to craft a wise Christian response to the changed situation.

Here, in summary, is the sharpest point I can put on the challenge of postmodernism and what it means for today's Christians. I mentioned in the second chapter that a rejection of authority drove the shift from premodernism to modernism. Moderns found themselves rejecting authority in politics, religion, and intellectual life. The shift from modernism to postmodernism never lost that impetus; postmoderns are as anti-authority as any modern, perhaps more so. But they have lost the faith that sustained modernism, the faith that human reason could deliver answers and find solutions to the great questions of human life.

We should ask, however, why modernism rejected authority to the extent that it did. And why has postmodernism kept rejecting authority, even in areas that moderns never dreamed of: linguistic meaning, moral absolutes, historical truth? The answer is that moderns and postmoderns are both in search of freedom. Admirably, at their best they desire this freedom not just for themselves as individuals, but for everyone. Modernism sought an individualistic autonomy for everyone, and one of the hallmarks of postmodernism, you will have noticed, is a fierce antipathy to anything that might oppress someone. Moderns and postmoderns alike hope to find freedom, though they conceive it differently, through eliminating constraints. Moderns were mainly concerned about fairly obvious constraints on behavior, those imposed by priests and kings. Postmoderns are more troubled by the subtler constraints that societies inscribe in your mind. Thus, they reject the softer authority of linguistic usage, of historical accounts, of morality, of science. For moderns, the antithesis of freedom is slavery, as represented in Sauron's Mordor in *Lord of the Rings;* for postmoderns, the antithesis of freedom is thought control, as in *The Matrix.* Whichever way freedom is understood, though, the pursuit of it drives both modernism and postmodernism.

In contrast, Christianity is fundamentally at odds with the project of seeking human freedom by eliminating constraints, whether the constraints are political, social, intellectual, or moral. For Christians understand themselves *both* as under the all-encompassing authority of God, who lays claim to every sphere of life, and *also* as supremely free, freer than any non-Christian could be. We do not often put it to ourselves like that, but every orthodox branch of Christianity would endorse it. And yet this double claim strikes contemporary Christians as deeply paradoxical—how can I be genuinely free and under authority at the same time? I suggest that we find this so deeply paradoxical precisely because we have grown up in a modern and postmodern climate of thought.

So here is the nub of the issue between Christianity and postmodernism: what is freedom? In particular, for a Christian, what exactly is this freedom we have, which yet submits to so great an authority as God? And what does it mean, what ramifications and consequences does it have, for Christian life? In particular, what does Christian freedom mean for those areas under pressure from postmodernism: morality, truth, knowledge, culture, and several others mentioned throughout this book? Well-articulated answers to these questions would go a long way toward providing a reasoned and sophisticated Christian response to the postmodern worldview.

The Rock and the Anchor

The tides of human culture have always been as changeable as the sea—placid at times, stormy at others. The present transition to postmodernism is on the stormy side. The Bible, however, gives us images of God as "the Rock eternal,"[1] and of the gospel as "an anchor for the soul, firm and secure."[2] Although the way God reveals himself and his message to each generation may differ, God himself does not change, nor does the good news he offers us in Jesus Christ. In this new time of our culture, with new threats and new challenges and new opportunities, God's promises remain secure. That is the most important knowledge to carry into the postmodern world.

For Further Thought

1. What's your final take on postmodernism? To use categories from the first chapter, are you morally concerned, evangelistically concerned, or theologi-

cally concerned? (Or uninterested?) Has your attitude changed, and why?

2. Did any of the historical references in this chapter strike you as eye-opening? If so, why?

3. How do you think of freedom? How does freedom relate to God's authority?

4. What, in your opinion, is the proper attitude for a Christian to have toward postmodernism?

Notes

Why Read about Postmodernism?

1. Obviously, "modern" here is something of a technical term. What happened was this: in the eighteenth century and after, historians began honoring the period in which they lived as "the modern period," contrasting it with the "ancient" world of the Greeks and Romans. (In between these two eras, unsurprisingly, came the so-called Middle Ages.) Now, with "postmodern," we've run out of adjectives.

Premodern and Modern Minds

1. Galileo also rejected the Aristotelian metaphysical view that ordinary objects were a compound of matter and form. For an Aristotelian, a loaf of bread is composed of matter, but it is also composed of attributes like the loaf's weight, its shape, and its color. Unifying all these is a form, bread itself, which is something other than either the matter or the attributes of the bread. Galileo's explanations appealed only to the matter in objects, and he dispensed with the notion of form. This made him a *materialist*. Materialism, however, is incompatible with the Catholic doctrine of the Eucharist, and recent evidence from Vatican archives suggests that Galileo's teachings may have been condemned for this reason as well.

The Postmodern Turn against Reason

1. E. B. Tylor, *Primitive Culture* (New York: Harper and Row, 1958), 1:26.

Truth, Power, and Morality

1. 1 Corinthians 11:5–6.

The Self

1. Or the Spirit proceeds from both the Father and the Son. This is a theological difference between Eastern and Western Christians.

Language and Thought

1. Jacques Derrida, in an interview published as "Between Brackets I" in *Points . . . : Interviews 1974–1994*, ed. Elisabeth Weber, trans. Peggy Kamuf et al. (Stanford, CA: Stanford University Press, 1995), 18.

Inquiry and Interpretation

1. 1 Corinthians 2:14.
2. Baruch Spinoza, *Theological-Political Treatise*, 2nd ed., trans. Samuel Shirley (Indianapolis, IN: Hackett, 1991).
3. 2 Timothy 3:16.
4. John 17:21.
5. This is the *metanarrative* of the Bible. We'll get to the concept of a metanarrative in chapter 9.

Culture and Irony

1. William R. Bright, "Foreword," in *The New Evidence that Demands a Verdict*, by Josh McDowell (Nashville, TN: Thomas Nelson, 1999), xi.

History and Hope

1. Friedrich Nietzsche, *Beyond Good and Evil*, I.38, in *Basic Writings of Nietzsche*, trans. and ed. Walter Kaufmann (New York: Random House, 1992), 239.
2. 1 Corinthians 15:19.

Epilogue

1. Isaiah 26:4.
2. Hebrews 6:19.

For Further Reading

Many books and articles about postmodernism have been published in the last ten years or so. What follows is a small selection of them in the form of an annotated bibliography, organized around the chapters of the book. Sometimes a single book is mentioned in multiple chapters where it would be relevant.

Why Read about Postmodernism?

George Marsden, *Fundamentalism and American Culture*. Traces the origin of the evangelical wing of American Christianity.

Charles Colson, *How Now Shall We Live?* Colson sets out a comprehensive Christian worldview, offering no olive branches to postmodernism or secularism. A prime exponent of the "moral concern" about postmodernism in many short articles and talks.

Leonard Sweet, *Soul Tsunami, AquaChurch,* and *Soul Salsa*. These three books (among several others by Sweet) suggest ways that the church in the twenty-first century can and must adapt to a postmodern culture. If you're attracted to the "evangelistic concern," Sweet is your man.

Brian McLaren, *A New Kind of Christian* and *A Generous Orthodoxy*. Rethinking Christianity in light of postmodernism. McLaren is at the forefront of the "Emerging Church" movement, which best expresses the "theological concern." He has written several other books as well. You might also be interested in the Web site www.emergingchurch .org.

J. Richard Middleton and Brian Walsh, *Truth Is Stranger Than It Used to Be: Biblical Faith in a Postmodern Age*. A basically postmodern-friendly book by the authors of *The Transforming Vision*.

Millard J. Erickson, *Truth or Consequences: The Promise and Perils of Postmodernism*. An evenhanded attempt at assessing postmodernism from an evangelical perspective.

David S. Dockery, *The Challenge of Postmodernism,* 2nd ed. A collection of essays by evangelical thinkers, spanning the gamut of opinions about postmodernism.

Douglas Groothius, *Truth Decay: Defending Christianity against the Challenges of Postmodernism*. Groothius upholds absolute truth against postmodern challenges.

Premodern and Modern Minds

Norman Cantor, *The Civilization of the Middle Ages*. The standard textbook on medieval history. Cantor has written many other works on the medieval era as well.

Diarmaid MacCulloch, *The Reformation: A History*. A recent and helpful survey of Reformation history.

Alister McGrath, *The Intellectual Origins of the European Reformation*. The title is self-explanatory; the chapters on scripture and the church are most relevant.

Immanuel Kant, "An Answer to the Question, 'What is Enlightenment?'" Kant's little essay is a nice introduction to the ideals of the Enlightenment. The essay, along with many other representative short pieces from the period, can be found in Isaac Kramnick, ed., *The Portable Enlightenment Reader*. For a more in-depth treatment of this historical period, consult Peter Gay, *The Enlightenment: An Interpretation*.

John Stuart Mill, *On Liberty*. This short tract sets out a theory of liberty that is recognizably our own and provides the original defense for the "free marketplace of ideas."

The Postmodern Turn against Reason

Rudyard Kipling, "The White Man's Burden." A classic statement of belief in European superiority, to be exercised benevolently.

Friedrich Nietzsche, *Twilight of the Idols*. I have found the short section, "How the 'True' World Became a Fable" particularly thought-provoking.

Richard Rorty, *Contingency, Irony, and Solidarity*. A clear statement from an optimistic postmodern. Rorty is easily the most readable influential postmodern thinker. Many of his essays are relevant, including "Science and Solidarity" in *Objectivity, Relativism, and Truth: Philosophical Papers*, vol. 1. You can get a sense for his take on many postmodern thinkers from the essays in *Essays on Heidegger and Others: Philosophical Papers*, vol. 2.

Jean-Francois Lyotard, *The Postmodern Condition*. A more pessimistic diagnosis of postmodernity. Hard to follow at times.

Thomas Kuhn, *The Structure of Scientific Revolutions*. An important work in the philosophy of science, which broke the image of science as a sphere of perfect knowledge.

Alan Sokal and Jean Bricmont, *Fashionable Nonsense: Postmodern Intellectuals' Abuse of Science*. A hard-hitting defense of modern ideals of scientific objectivity against postmodern criticisms.

Stanley Grenz, *A Primer on Postmodernism*. Excellent introduction to postmodernism, written by a theologian.

Steven Connor, ed., *The Cambridge Companion to Postmodernism*. Academic flavor.

Richard Kearney, *Modern Movements in European Philosophy*. Provides short sketches of the philosophies of a number of postmodern thinkers and the philosophers who influenced them most.

Hans Bertens and Joseph Natoli, eds., *Postmodernism: The Key Figures*. Short treatments of fifty-three postmodern thinkers, writers, and artists.

Walter Truett Anderson, *The Truth About the Truth*. A collection of short, readable pieces on a variety of themes in postmodernism. Two other helpful books by Anderson (not collections) are *Reality Isn't What It Used to Be* and *All Connected Now: Life in the First Global Civilization*.

Truth, Power, and Morality

Ruth Benedict, "A Defense of Moral Relativism." Written by a prominent anthropologist.

John Hospers, "The Problem with Relativism." A reply to Benedict.

Friedrich Nietzsche, *Beyond Good and Evil* and *The Genealogy of Morals.* Morality is a plot by the weak to control the strong. Be strong.

Richard Rorty, "Postmodern Bourgeois Liberalism." Eye-opening for its frank disavowal of any intrinsic human dignity to individuals.

Michel Foucault, *Discipline and Punish.* Delineates differences in punishment between the premodern and modern periods; suggests that modernity was more all-encompassingly coercive than premodernity ever aspired to be. This is the easiest of Foucault's many books to read. There is also a whole industry devoted to Foucault commentary. You might also check out the interviews collected in *Power/Knowledge.*

Isaiah Berlin, "The Pursuit of the Ideal," in *The Crooked Timber of Humanity.* A reflective, semi-autobiographical essay arguing for the acknowledgment of a plurality of genuine but irreconcilable values.

Jacques Derrida, "Force of Law: The 'Mystical Foundation of Authority,'" in Drucilla Cornell et al., eds., *Deconstruction and the Possibility of Justice.* An influential but difficult essay. Derrida's later period is marked by a more religious turn; see, for example, *Schibboleth.* Derrida/Caputo, *Deconstruction in a Nutshell,* is a helpful (and easier) introduction to Derrida's thought, early and late.

John Caputo, *Against Ethics.* A postmodern critique of the (doomed) enterprise of moral theorizing. You might also want to look at *The Tears and Prayers of Jacques Derrida,* which grapples with the "religious turn" in Derrida's philosophy.

Simon Critchley, *The Ethics of Deconstruction.* A different view of ethics from a postmodern perspective.

The Self

Benjamin Franklin, *Autobiography,* and Ralph Waldo Emerson, "Self-Reliance." Two classic modern pictures of the self.

Michel Foucault, "What is Enlightenment?" and "The Ethic of the Concern for the Self as a Practice of Freedom." These essays shed light on a prominent postmodern's view of the self and how it is to be shaped. Much of Foucault's later work concentrates on this theme.

Kenneth Gergen, *The Saturated Self: Dilemmas of Identity in Contemporary Life*. A psychologist analyzes the effects of postmodernity. Very helpful and easy to follow; emphasizes the social and cultural (rather than intellectual) roots of postmodernity.

Sherry Turkle, *The Second Self: Computers and the Human Spirit*. Explores the ways that familiarity with computers changes our image of ourselves.

Alasdair MacIntyre, "The Virtues, the Unity of a Human Life, and the Concept of a Tradition," chapter 15 in the very influential *After Virtue*. MacIntyre argues against the postmodern view of a fragmented, socially constructed self.

Richard Rorty, "The Contingency of Selfhood," chapter 2 in *Contingency, Irony, and Solidarity*.

Walter Truett Anderson, *The Future of the Self*. Explores postmodern possibilities for human living. Anderson is a booster for postmodernism. Also check out his *The Truth about the Truth*, especially Part Three, "Self, Sex and Sanity."

Calvin O. Schrag, *The Self after Postmodernity*.

Stanley Hauerwas, *The Church as Polis*. Argues for the character-shaping function of the church. Hauerwas has defended the church's role as a counterculture in many places; one of the more popular is *Resident Aliens*, coauthored with William H. Willimon.

Language and Thought

Friedrich Nietzsche, "On Truth and Lies in a Non-Moral Sense." An early essay arguing that concepts are abstractions from experience and therefore falsehoods.

Benjamin Lee Whorf, "Science and Linguistics," in John Carroll, ed., *Language, Thought, and Reality: Selected Writings*. Advances what came to be known as the "Sapir-Whorf hypothesis," that language deeply influences thought.

Richard Rorty, "The Contingency of Language," chapter 1 in *Contingency, Irony, and Solidarity*.

Jacques Derrida, "Structure, Sign and Play in the Discourse of the Human Sciences." A seminal essay that argues against any ultimate source of meaning. Difficult. Many other works by Derrida are relevant as well: his first book, *Of Grammatology,* and the essays collected in *Writing and Difference* especially. *Points* is a collection of interviews and an easy way into the muddy waters of deconstruction. Not to be despised is Jim Powell, *Derrida for Beginners,* an easy-to-digest, comic-book presentation of an otherwise formidable thinker. (There is also a *Nietzsche,* a *Foucault,* and a *Lacan for Beginners.*)

Ludwig Wittgenstein, *Philosophical Investigations.* For advanced or masochistic readers only. Advances the "game" view of language. Compare it to Plato's *Cratylus,* where words are names of things, or John Locke's *An Essay Concerning Human Understanding,* where words are names of ideas in the mind.

Inquiry and Interpretation

Jean Leclercq, *The Love of Learning and the Desire for God: A Study of Monastic Culture.* Gives a great sense of the approach to knowledge in the Middle Ages.

Max Weber, "Science as a Vocation." Important essay by a famous sociologist.

Jean-Francois Lyotard, *The Postmodern Condition.* Examines "the question of knowledge" and concludes that the main thing is to foster intellectual instability by continuing to have new ideas.

Roland Barthes, "Death of the Author" and "From Work to Text." These important short essays by a prominent French literary theorist lay out a postmodern view of "texts." See also Michel Foucault, "What is an Author?" A good collection on this topic is Josué V. Harari, ed., *Textual Strategies: Perspectives in Post-Structuralist Criticism.*

Mark Taylor, *Erring: A Postmodern A/theology.* Applies postmodern ideas to religious thought. Not too worried about orthodoxy.

A. K. M. Adam, ed., *Handbook of Postmodern Biblical Interpretation.* Reference work with useful essays.

Gavin Hyman, *The Predicament of Postmodern Theology: Radical Orthodoxy or Nihilist Textualism?* One among many good books grappling with theology in a postmodern context. See the whole Brazos Press catalog for more.

Culture and Irony

Walter Truett Anderson, *All Connected Now: Life in the First Global Civilization.*

Anthony Giddens, *Runaway World: How Globalization Is Reshaping Our Lives*. See also his *The Consequences of Modernity* and the book of essays he edited with Will Hutton, *Global Capitalism*. Giddens has written many other insightful books as well.

Jim Collins, *Uncommon Cultures: Popular Culture and Post-modernism*.

James Davison Hunter, *Culture Wars: The Struggle to Define America*. Hunter invented the term "culture wars" in this book.

Richard Rorty, *Contingency, Irony, and Solidarity*, especially chapters 3–6.

David Harvey, *The Condition of Postmodernity: An Enquiry into the Origins of Cultural Change*. An analysis of postmodern culture—he doesn't like it—from a Marxist perspective. In the same vein, see Terry Eagleton, *The Illusions of Postmodernism,* and Frederic Jameson, *Postmodernism, or the Cultural Logic of Late Capitalism*.

History and Hope

Peter Novick, *That Noble Dream: The "Objectivity Question" and the American Historical Profession*. The history of the discipline of history, relating the rise and fall of objectivity as a professional ideal.

Hayden White, "The Historical Text as Literary Artifact." History writing is more about rhetorical structures than about recitation of facts. White's *Metahistory* is the large-scale presentation of this argument.

Alasdair MacIntyre, "The Virtues, the Unity of a Human Life, and the Concept of a Tradition," chapter 15 in *After Virtue*. Among other things, a reply to White.

Jean-Francois Lyotard, *The Postmodern Condition*. Introduced the notion of metanarrative.

J. Richard Middleton and Brian Walsh, *Truth Is Stranger Than It Used to Be: Biblical Faith in a Postmodern Age*. Maps a way of thinking about a Christian worldview as a metanarrative.

Epilogue

Václav Havel, "The Philadelphia Liberty Medal Speech." Though we live in a postmodern world, we can't do without the modern notion of human rights. We have to ground morality in something transcendent.

Alasdair MacIntyre, *After Virtue*. An influential diagnosis of the post-modern condition and an advocate for a premodern prescription. MacIntyre's later works, including *Three Rival Versions of Moral Enquiry* and *Whose Justice? Which Rationality?* continue the theme.

John Paul II, *The Splendor of Truth*. This papal encyclical presents a firm Christian response to postmodern skepticism and relativism.

John Milbank, ed., *Radical Orthodoxy: A New Theology*. This collection of essays is the flagship publication for the postmodern theological movement called Radical Orthodoxy. Other works in the RO vein are Milbank's *Theology and Social Theory: Beyond Secular Reason* and books by Catherine Pickstock and Graham Ward. For an introduction to the movement, see James K. A. Smith, *Introducing Radical Orthodoxy: Mapping a Post-secular Theology*.